THE TRANSITION OF YOUTH TO ADULTHOOD: A BRIDGE TOO LONG

THE TRANSITION OF YOUTH TO ADULTHOOD: A BRIDGE TOO LONG

A Report to Educators, Sociologists, Legislators, and Youth Policymaking Bodies

National Commission on Youth
B. Frank Brown, Director
Established by the Charles F. Kettering Foundation

Westview Press / Boulder, Colorado

The interpretations and conclusions contained in this publication represent the views of the National Commission on Youth and not necessarily those of the Kettering Foundation or its trustees or officers.

Published in 1980 in the United States of America by
  Westview Press, Inc.
  5500 Central Avenue
  Boulder, Colorado 80301
  Frederick A. Praeger, Publisher

Library of Congress Cataloging in Publication Data
National Commission on Youth.
  The transition of youth to adulthood: a bridge too long.
  1. Youth policy – United States – Addresses, essays, lectures. 2. Conflict of generations – Addresses, essays, lectures. 3. Adulthood – Addresses, essays, lectures.
I. Title.
HQ796.N3133 1980   301.43'15   79-20049
ISBN 0-89158-675-X
ISBN 0-89158-756-X pbk.

Printed and bound in the United States of America

CONTENTS

v

80-5725

Part 2
Needs of Youth

Part 3
Assessing Youth Policy

Part 4
Evolving Youth Policy

ACKNOWLEDGMENTS

The Charles F. Kettering Foundation expresses appreciation to the following individuals who responsibly and diligently served as members of the National Commission on Youth giving guidance and direction to the development of this report:

Gordon T. Bowden
Director, Educational Relations
American Telephone & Telegraph Company
New York, New York

Urie Bronfenbrenner
Professor, Department of Human Development and Family Studies
Cornell University
Ithaca, New York

James Coleman, *Chairman of the Commission*
Professor, Department of Sociology
University of Chicago
Chicago, Illinois

Robert A. Davies
Vice President, Corporate Strategy
Armco Steel Corporation
Middletown, Ohio

Walter Davis
Director, Department of Education
AFL-CIO
Washington, D.C.

Dennis Gallagher
Associate Executive Director
National Manpower Institute
Washington, D.C.

George Gallup
Chairman, The Gallup Poll
American Institute of Public Opinion
Princeton, New Jersey

Willis W. Harman
Director, Educational Policy Research Center
Stanford Research Institute
Menlo Park, California

Robert T. McGee
Superintendent
Denton Independent School District
Denton, Texas

Anthony J. Moffett
Congressman
Sixth District, Connecticut
Washington, D.C.

William J. Saunders
Executive Assistant to the Superintendent
Public Schools of the District of Columbia
Washington, D.C.

Mildred K. Wurf
Coordinator
National Collaboration for Youth
Washington, D.C.

Ex Officio: Samuel G. Sava
Vice President and Special Assistant to the President
Charles F. Kettering Foundation
Dayton, Ohio

*The Commission expresses its special appreciation to
Dr. David L. Manning. To him went the task
of pulling together the Commission's ideas, organizing
the tapes, compiling the notes, and distilling two years
of information into written form.*

INTRODUCTION

Perhaps the greatest challenge facing American society is the creation of new environments for youth. These new situations must be based upon a richer mix between youth and adults.

The family stands almost alone, weakly assisted by the teacher-student relationship, in supporting a framework of communication between the young and the old. The relationship of child to parent carries nearly the entire responsibility for cross-age communication. This paucity of youth/adult contacts makes the transition to adulthood a long and complex process.

Ralph Tyler, a distinguished scholar in American education for over fifty years, states the implications of separating youth from adults as follows:

> The net result of this forced isolation has been to alienate young people from the adult society, to delay personal and social maturation, sometimes to inhibit permanently the development of responsibility because of overprotection from the consequence of personal actions.
>
> American society cannot long endure without a means for a peaceful and effective transition of youth into adulthood.*

This report constitutes a search for new environments for youth that will bring them into frequent, realistic contact with adults. The intent is to find a more effective way of bridging the gap between youth and adulthood.

The purpose of this new environmental mix is to provide youth with action-rich experiences designed to develop more effectively their capacities for managing their own affairs in a complex and changing world.

It is well established that the peer group is an inappropriate source for developing adult goals; yet the process of age grading in schools perpetuates a way of life in which young speak mostly to each other.

*Ralph W. Tyler, "Tomorrow's Education," *American Education*, U.S. Department of HEW, Office of Education, August-September 1975, p. 17.

This type of institutionalization nurtures the development of a youth counterculture and hinders the transmission of knowledge from generation to generation.

Sociologist Elise Boulding of the University of Colorado describes succinctly the inimical effects of age grading: "Age grading means that toddlers will be kept with toddlers; kindergarteners with kindergarteners; elementary, junior high, and senior high with each other; college and young married with their own; young parents with one another; middle years and retirees and golden-age folk with their own."

Age groups are wired together so tightly in school and society that, as Dean George Gerbner has said, "one short circuit will fry them all."

The report is unique. It embraces a comprehensive approach to the problems of youth. Unquestionably, many of the recommendations will spark controversy. This is not unintended. It is the Commission's hope that this report will initiate spirited, thoughtful public debate that will culminate in the development of a national youth policy.

B. Frank Brown
Director
National Commission on Youth

RECOMMENDATIONS FOR IMPROVING THE TRANSITION OF YOUTH TO ADULTHOOD

In this complex contemporary culture, it is unrealistic to expect any institution to be the exclusive environment for the transition of youth to adulthood. Yet society relies very heavily on the secondary school as the major institution to accomplish this task. Clearly, secondary schools need assistance.

The report of the National Commission on Youth is directed to the institutions and parties that must play an integral role in attempts to design new environments for youth. The recommendations are presented in summarized form here and substantiated in detail in the ensuing chapters. No importance should be attached to their numerical designation; they are presented in the order in which they appear in the report.

Recommendation 1: Designing New Environments for Youth. High schools should become action-rich institutions. To achieve this objective, schools must develop heretofore neglected relationships with community-based institutions. High schools can no longer function as the pervasive or exclusive environment for the transition of youth to adulthood.

Recommendation 2: Developing Community-Based Educational Programs. Schools should develop imaginative, community-based programs in order to bring educational opportunities to youth on a dispersed, convenient basis. A future goal of all schools should be to make use of the community so that youth are allowed to function not as passive students but as active contributors to the community. The high schools in particular must play a coordinating role in the design and development of community-based programs. The intent is to break down the barriers that presently exist between the school and the community, thereby ensuring a better mix between youth and adults in the transitional process.

1

Recommendation 3: Credit for Community-Based Education. Secondary schools should award academic credit for successful learning experiences in those community-based programs that aid students in mastering basic knowledge areas and skills.

Recommendation 4: Creation of a National Youth Service. The Congress of the United States should establish a National Youth Service guaranteeing all American youth the opportunity for at least one year of full-time service to their community or to the nation.

All youth, male and female alike, between the ages of sixteen and twenty-one should be guaranteed the opportunity to participate for at least one year of full-time service in the program; all youth between the ages of fourteen and twenty-one would be eligible for part-time participation in National Youth Service programs as part of school-related cooperative programs. Part-time service would be rendered in one's own community; full-time participation would most likely entail service in distant locations.

Recommendation 5: Mandatory Registration for National Youth Service. Congress should enact legislation *requiring* all American citizens, both male and female, at the age of eighteen to register for the opportunity to participate in a National Youth Service program. Mandatory registration will assure that all eighteen-year-olds receive counseling and guidance in relation to National Youth Service opportunities and values.

Youth transitional planning councils should be designated as the mechanism through which compulsory registration is accomplished. In the event that there is no youth transitional planning council operating on the local level, registration of participants should take place through the local Selective Service office.

Recommendation 6: Advocating National Youth Service Experience as a Condition of Employment. All employers – individuals, agencies, institutions, and businesses – should encourage youth to register and participate in the National Youth Service experience. Employers should advocate at least one year of service experience as a prerequisite for employment.

Recommendation 7: Educational Entitlements. Serious consideration should be given to incorporating an educational entitlement voucher – a type of GI Bill of Rights for service – into any plan for National Youth Service. Opportunity vouchers should grant one year of educational entitlement for each year of service experience up to a maximum of four years.

Recommendation 8: Establishing Youth Transitional Planning Councils on the Local Level. Youth transitional planning councils should be developed in every community to smooth, shorten, and enhance the transition of youth to adulthood. Communities that are unable to sustain councils for lack of numbers or resources should establish regional councils.

Recommendation 9: Membership and Status of Youth Transitional Planning Councils. The mayor or chief executive of the community should appoint a cross-section of interested citizens to the youth transitional planning council. The council should be granted legal status and stand autonomous from local school boards.

Recommendation 10: Youth Unemployment Policies. The focus of government policies to reduce youth unemployment should be twofold. Short-term policy initiatives should concentrate on the *cyclical* and *frictional* aspects of youth unemployment in order to ameliorate undue suffering and hardship among unemployed youth, while longterm policies should focus on the *structural* aspects of youth unemployment in order to reduce persistently high rates of unemployment among the young.

Recommendation 11: Payment of a Differentiated Wage to Youth in Training. Payment of less than minimum wage should be made to youth who are gaining job training and experience in apprenticeships, internships, and job-training programs.

Payment of a subminimum wage to youth in training can create incentives for private employers to develop and expand carefully supervised programs.

Performance-based training grants, tax write-offs, and wage tax deferments can provide additional incentives to stimulate training programs in the private sector.

Recommendation 12: Improvement of Youth Employment Services. The Bureau of Labor Statistics should take steps to develop more reliable statistical data on the scope of youth unemployment.

Concomitantly, state governments should develop local and regional data that reflect more accurately the rate of youth unemployment in local settings and among different concentrations of youth.

Along with these efforts, the U.S. Employment Service should establish a youth section to better serve the employment needs of young people.

Recommendation 13: Revision of Child Labor Laws. Federal and state governments should launch a coordinated effort under the U.S. Department of Labor to revise the entire body of child labor law. Such revision is needed to better safeguard the health of young people on the job and to open up additional avenues of employment through the deletion of antiquated statutes and regulations.

Recommendation 14: Television Violence. The viewing public should continue to pressure the television networks and their local affiliates to assume increased responsibility for decreasing the levels of crime and violence on television to which youth are exposed.

Recommendation 15: Reform of the Juvenile Justice System. The present system of juvenile justice should be reconstituted along new lines. The key is to differentiate within the existing system.

Courts should continue their efforts to separate serious offenders from less serious offenders. The use of nonincarcerative sanctions – fines, restitutions, community service – should be encouraged for less serious offenses.

Finally, if rehabilitation is the primary objective of the juvenile justice system, a wide array of remedial services must be provided to meet the needs of youthful offenders.

Recommendation 16: Prevention of Youth Crime and Delinquency. Efforts to prevent youth crime and delinquency should focus on early levels of intervention and diversion. Preventive measures will have maximum impact when they are brought to bear on the environments in which youth operate – the home, the school, the neighborhood, and the community. Whenever feasible, youth offenders should render an appropriate form of service to the neighborhood or to the community as a form of restitution for criminal offenses.

Recommendation 17: Elimination of Status Offender Classification. The courts should cease the practice of classifying youth as status offenders. The jurisdiction of the juvenile court system should be limited to those acts that if committed by an adult, would constitute a criminal offense and to dependent and neglect statutes, which allow the courts to intervene in order to protect the health and welfare of young people.

Recommendation 18: Development of Improved Health-Care Delivery Systems. The medical profession should take steps to develop improved health-care delivery systems for young people. Health-care services can be built into the organizational structure of community-based organizations, such as the Boys' Clubs, which serve large and diverse numbers of youth.

Health programs that are participatory and continuing rather than passive and informational should be developed in secondary schools. The object of these programs should be to ensure that before leaving high school all young persons have an understanding of the nature of human reproduction and the dangers of smoking, drug abuse, and alcohol.

Recommendation 19: Youth Transitional Planning Councils as Policy-making Bodies. Mayors, acting as youth advocates, should designate and utilize youth transitional planning councils as mechanisms to develop youth policies and programs on the local level.

Recommendation 20: Federal and State Guidelines to Local Communities. Federal and state policy guidelines to local communities should be prescriptive, not restrictive, in character. The purpose of such guidelines should be to establish a nominal amount of monitoring of youth programs, to provide leadership, and to create incentives for organizations and individuals who serve youth on the local level.

Recommendation 21: Development of Youth Policy at the State Level. Each state governor should appoint a cabinet-level special assistant for youth affairs. This would enable states to coordinate more effectively existing youth policies and programs, to design policies and programs for youth where they do not presently exist, and to articulate a coherent youth policy on the state level.

Recommendation 22: Development of a Comprehensive National Youth Policy. A youth policy should be developed at the federal level to serve the needs of all young persons rather than a targeted segment of the youth population. This national youth policy should be long-term in nature to allow several years start-up time in youth programs and permit the buildup of experienced personnel for effective program supervision. Implementation would include encouragement of local efforts to apply national policies in creative ways.

Recommendation 23: Transition Schools. Transition schools should be established for the final years of secondary education. These would offer high school students a wide variety of options to enable them to move beyond the classroom into the neighborhood and the community to complete their education. Transition schools, *operated by the public school system,* would afford youth opportunities to pursue special interests, to explore career options, to learn new skills, and to test newly acquired competencies in internships and apprenticeships in a community-based environment.

Recommendation 24: Optional Learning Centers. Optional learning centers should be established to serve as safety nets for youth who find transition schools inappropriate for their educational needs. *Operating independently of the public school system,* optional learning centers would provide jobs, service opportunities, and vocational apprenticeships in the community. Youth transitional planning councils would be responsible for the placement of students in jobs and for monitoring their progress in field-work settings.

Recommendation 25: Vocational Education in a Community-Based Environment. Vocational education should be shifted from the high schools into the community, where it more properly belongs. The concept of performance contracting should be revived to monitor the learning of apprentice and vocational skills that are taught by community-based institutions.

Recommendation 26: A Presidential Commission to Study Youth Problems. A presidential commission should be established to study the social, economic, and political conditions from which arise the problems of youth. Focusing on these larger issues, the recommendations of the commission would serve as a philosophical anchor point for Congress to legislate specific laws and mechanisms to facilitate the transition of youth to adulthood.

Recommendation 27: A White House Youth Office to Coordinate Policies and Programs. A White House youth office should be established to coordinate more effectively the present horizontal approach to policymaking and program implementation. Operating under presidential mandate, the youth office would be empowered to coordinate all youth-related policies, programs, and budgetary decisions. This vertical dimension should result in more effective decision-making procedures and give much-needed visibility to youth affairs on the national level.

PART 1

TRANSITION OF YOUTH

1

YOUTH IN TRANSITION

Recommendation 1: Designing New Environments for Youth. *High schools should become action-rich institutions. To achieve this objective, schools must develop heretofore neglected relationships with community-based institutions. High schools can no longer function as the pervasive or exclusive environment for the transition of youth to adulthood.*

The transition periods in human development are receiving increasing attention. We are avidly taking our own pulses and sorting out the tangible and intangible factors that influence our directions. Through various creative approaches, we are attempting to ease on down the road.

The transition from youth to adulthood has never been easy. (For purposes of this report, *youth* are defined as persons between the ages of fourteen and twenty-one. However, it is imperative to recognize that this is not a homogeneous group in which all face similar problems, have similar needs, and require similar program intervention. Instead, the group encompasses a wide latitude of needs, interests, and behaviors.) Contemporary youth move in a society far different from that of their peers several centuries ago. The pace of learning is quicker. Sexual maturity arrives earlier. And yet, through a combination of many factors, youth are held back and shielded from the adult world. The bridge of time between youth and adulthood has become a bridge too long.

The transition of youth to adulthood is difficult even in the best of times. But this is the worst of times for significant numbers of American youth. Many of the traditional institutions that assist youth to adulthood are changing, crumbling, and even collapsing. The decline of the family unit is well documented. Beleaguered school systems are attacked from all sides—by students, parents, and employers—for their failure to teach marketable skills to the young. Governmental bodies on all levels remain largely unresponsive to the serious plight of youth.

In this report the National Commission on Youth hopes to generate widespread discussion and debate on a variety of topics, many controversial in nature, for the purpose of shortening the transition to adulthood for American youth. The recommendations in the report are the products of intensive scrutiny and prolonged debate over matters characterized by complexity and turbulence (Appendix A). Some of the Commission's recommendations are controversial. But controversy is the cutting edge of progress.

The times may seem singularly inappropriate for the announcement of far-reaching recommendations involving fundamental changes in institutional forms and practices. Admittedly, the nation is in a period of conservatism.

And today's educational credos – "back to basics" and "competency-based" education – are important aspects of education. Basic literacy is the essential ingredient in the solution for most youth transition problems and achieving it may be one of our more difficult problems. The fundamentally serious problems of maintaining learning motivation and achievement standards are bound up with reading, writing, and computation abilities (including a new need for computer literacy), and these problems, which are not being solved very well, may account more than anything else for what we call youth maturity problems. Yet, these two credos are inadequate solutions. The need for more aggressive action is almost a moral imperative. In justice to the nation's greatest resource for the future – our youth – the Commission presents these recommendations.

Because the goal of the Commission is to design wholly new contexts for the transition of youth to adulthood, it must necessarily call to action all segments of the nation. The recommendations are obviously too ambitious to be accomplished exclusively through the actions of any single sector or institution. Collective effort is required. Joint responsibility must be shared by both private and public sectors, encompassing federal, state, and local levels.

Every generation of adults tries to share the benefits of its hard-won wisdom with the young. Although the incremental wisdom of the past, by itself, never suffices to solve present problems, we do benefit from the past. We must utilize our expertise so that in the future the transition time is shorter. The future is now.

Some youth find the future is never. For them, America has become a nation turned upside down. Society has cast them into a state of limbo. There they are held in a stage of dependency on adults and are increasingly denied opportunities for productive labor. Ironically, they are blocked from attaining responsibility by the policies of the very institutions that are supposed to shape their lives for the better.

What is the cost of this malaise to young people? For many, it means a socioeconomic death at an early age, and once the will to strive and attain has been destroyed, it is death in a spiritual sense as well.

Unemployment is rapidly becoming a way of life for many of the young.[1] About half of the unemployed in America are between the ages of sixteen and twenty-four, a disproportionate fraction of these being black or of other minority origins. Of this group, many have never had a job and have given up hope of ever finding one. Many have completed school without education, training, or practical know-how; they cannot compete successfully in the arena of life.

Other youth have the capabilities to make a significant contribution to society but are so "turned off" by the system that they have dropped out. The escape mechanisms they resort to in order to assuage their feelings of frustration have become a national tragedy. Drugs and alcohol have become a quick and easy fix to a fleeting moment of euphoria. Widespread use of such intoxicants in turn engenders delinquency and crime that exacerbate the problems of youth.

Another group of youth languishes in jails and similar types of incarcerating institutions. Many of these young people are simply unprepared for the transition to adulthood. An overwhelming percentage of them are illiterate. Violent and illegal acts are their way of gaining a measure of revenge against the system that imprisons them. Even at a relatively young age many have given up on America.

The frustration is even greater for a final group. It is estimated that one million youth run away from home each year. But action of this magnitude is overshadowed when juxtaposed with a final sobering statistic. Suicide is now the second leading cause of death for youth between ages fifteen and twenty-four. Regretfully, self-destruction has become an option exercised by increasing numbers of the young.

But statistics cannot adequately describe the long-range damage to the spiritual fabric of America when a substantial part of the population has no hope for a productive role in life.

What kind of society are we? On one hand, we worship youthfulness in our culture, raising it to cult status. But, on the other hand, we have, at this point in history, become impatient with our young.[2] Youth has become the siren-goddess of American society, simultaneously enthralling and tormenting us. For far too many of the young the only role they can envision is to fill the cracks and niches that remain open to them — constructive critic, hedonistic consumer, languid student, embittered victim, and degenerative dropout. Why complain?

The restiveness that characterized American youth of the sixties has all but vanished. As youth have turned inward, it has become a truism for adult America that this bodes well for the nation's future. But does it? Is this turning inward a harbinger of a more ominous trend? Is it not, in fact, confirmation of a shift in youth attitudes from a state of alienation and hostility to a state of hopelessness and despair toward the institutions – the family, the school, the marketplace, the government – that so intimately affect their lives?

How did we get where we are? A backward glance may give us some perspective.

Historical Evolution of the Transition to Adulthood

The continued vitality of a society depends on the degree of success it has in transforming its youth into productive adults. Societies develop institutions to assist in this socialization process. The Presidential Science Advisory Committee's report, entitled *Youth: Transition to Adulthood*, identified two distinct evolutionary periods in our history: "a *work phase* followed by a *schooling phase*."[3]

The initial *work phase* was based primarily on economic considerations. Young people were rushed into work roles as soon as they achieved a physical maturity commensurate to the job they were expected to perform. In this early period of American history, the economic productivity of the young was crucial, indeed imperative, to the financial well-being of the family. The dominant institutional influences on the young were the home and the workplace. No sharp lines of demarcation existed between the two. Socialization of the young during this period was a relatively simple process. Youth merely had to emulate the actions of parents.

As America transformed itself from an agrarian to an industrialized society, a whole new array of occupations was created. Many of these jobs were quite different from the occupations that existed in home workshops. At this point, the socialization process of youth to adulthood was characterized by a new phase – an extended *schooling phase* – designed to produce increased economic opportunity for the young. Direct access to economic productivity was now postponed for the young in the name of increased economic opportunity. Compulsory formal schooling, emphasizing cognitive learning skills, was viewed as a sine qua non for successful performance in the adult world of work. Institutional primacy for the school was ensured through the passage of a series of child labor laws and minimum wage standards. As a consequence, the school replaced the home and the workplace as the dominant socializing force in the lives of maturing youth.

Along with the rising importance of the school, there was a marked tendency in American society to grade and segregate the young by age. This tendency manifested itself in the classification and promotional practices of the school. Age became the major criterion for placement in grade levels. The promotional practices of the school quickly perpetuated the system from the primary grades through the secondary level. The social environment of maturing youth was now monopolized on a formal level by the school and informally by the age group.[4] The home, the church, and the community had been eclipsed as the major socializing forces on the young.

Fragmentization of the Transitional Process

The emergence of the school as the dominant institutional force in the lives of youth led to a diminution of the home, the church, and the community as settings where youth learned about the transition to adulthood. American society is now characterized by what Kurt Lewin calls "systems in abscission," that is, the various institutions function as isolated entities, cut off from each other. Present societal development is characterized by the progressive fragmentation and isolation of the socializing institutions. A tart observation of Commission member Urie Bronfenbrenner says it best: "We're all in disconnected pieces."[5]

The problems of youth are not rooted solely in the home, the school, or the workplace; they are rooted instead in the external society, which has undermined the capacity of these institutions to operate in optimum fashion. The real secret to successful change lies in focusing our efforts on the connections between these institutions. By severing these interconnections, we have isolated the institutions from each other. But it is precisely these interconnections that count most. Youth have become a kind of "lumpen proletariat," says Commissioner James Coleman, "separated from any institutional base."[6] Increased numbers of youth fall between the cracks in the institutional framework.

The Protection of Youth

In *The Leviathan,* Thomas Hobbes portrayed his world as nasty, mean, and brutish. The exploitation of the young in these circumstances was particularly acute. However, the civilizing influences of education, resulting in the passage of enlightened social legislation, have enabled Western civilization to shed a good deal of its Hobbesian flavor. Life need not be all sound and fury or, in Thoreau's term, "quiet desperation." Institutions were developed to protect the young. A condition of full parental authority was transformed gradually to one characterized by shared authority between parents and institutional agents, such as the school.[7]

In their zeal to protect youth from the vicissitudes of life, adults have unwittingly and ironically created a "Catch 22" system. Protection has come to mean isolation. Youth are now isolated, restrained, and eventually victimized by the very institutions designed for their protection.[8] Continued protection for youth remains a necessity. This goal should not be accomplished, however, by isolating youth from the real world.

The schools, as presently constituted, are useful illustrations of this phenomenon. As mentioned above, in this setting children are isolated from each other by grade levels on the basis of age rather than by levels of competencies. Promotional policies institutionalize this isolation. Further isolation occurs when the young are segregated (again on the basis of age) into primary, middle, and secondary divisions. As a consequence of this lack of interaction between the old and the young, there is little "trickle-down" learning.[9]

To fill this need for connections in the lives of youth, incidental and spontaneous structures of socialization such as books, films, and the media – especially television – develop in and around the formally constituted institutions.[10] As formal institutions inhibit and negate the purposes for which they were created, these incidental and spontaneous structures take on new importance. Ultimately they become no less important than the formal institutions themselves. The end result is that the civilizing process grows exceedingly complex for the young.

The implications of this trend are sobering and deserve careful analysis. A host of vexing questions must be considered: What are the environments in which youth can best grow into adults? How much institutional protection should be afforded youth in the transition to adulthood? What kinds of institutions are most appropriate to assist youth in the transitional process?

The Commission believes that the institutional framework for the transition of youth to adulthood is presently in need of serious repair and modernization. The need to create a symbiotic relationship between youth and the institutions to assist them in the transitional process is obvious. It is to this task that the Commission has given its attention.

A Starting Point: Schooling Versus Education

American education has traditionally operated on the premise that *schooling* is synonymous with *education*. Herein lies a problem.

As noted previously, in early America schooling was that part of education that occupied a relatively minor part of youth's lives. Little time was spent in the schoolhouse in a formal institutional setting. In this setting, schools taught the young basic academic skills. The three R s, honed by repetitious drills, were the backbone of formal schooling. The more functional parts of education – learning about work, learning how to be a competent husband or wife or father or mother, learning how to be a responsible and contributing member of a town – were acquired outside the schoolhouse.

With the absence of institutional barriers between the family, the school, and the workplace, schooling in a formal sense and education in an informal sense were regarded as equally important. Schooling and education were synonymous in the colonial mind. No priority existed between learning that occurred in the formal schoolhouse setting and what was learned in the informal setting of the community. Both were equal and integral parts of one's education.

As American society shed its agrarian beginnings, schooling and education evolved as separate functions. Youth were circumscribed from the workplace by legislation concerned with their protection. Formal schooling occupied increased segments of the lives of the young. Earning and learning were now separate entities in youth's lives.

If a more appropriate educational environment for the transition of youth to adulthood is to be prescribed, identifying the relationship of schooling and education is a necessary starting point. Schooling is only one part of education. The remaining parts, those aspects transpiring outside the school in an informal community setting, require as much explicit planning and organization as the formal aspects of the educational process.

Toward a New Transitional Phase

The time has come to develop a new transitional phase to assist youth to adulthood. Presently the school is the keystone of the transitional process. But societal dissatisfaction with the school's role in this process is rampant.

As presently constituted, schools offer an incomplete context for the transition of youth to adulthood. Traditionally, schools have emphasized self-centered objectives, focusing on the acquisition of cognitive skills and knowledge for personal growth. Cognitive skills and knowledge are crucial to growing up, not only because of the self-discipline required but also for their central role in most jobs in the world of work. In addition, however, youth need a broader environment to learn and practice their skills.

The new transitional phase includes schooling but in a changed capacity. In this new capacity the Commission recommends that schools function as a pervasive but not an exclusive environment for youth. Schooling is simply not an island unto itself. The real world, as represented by environments in which adults operate, must be tied more intimately to the formal school setting. Young people currently operate in environments that have become impoverished in their ability to provide concrete opportunities for responsible and productive action. Schools, in conjunction with other agencies, must become action-rich institutions, providing community-based learning experiences.

Retooling of such a fundamental nature requires rethinking even the most common aspects of the way in which institutions operate. The Commission is acutely aware of the necessity to design new environments that have broader objectives than those in which the school has traditionally operated. Educators must open the schoolhouse doors to the real world, stressing relationships between their students and adults in the community. The long-standing barrier between town and gown must be overcome with all due haste. No longer should schools insulate the young from the real world.

In addition to teaching the traditional objectives of acquiring skills and knowledge, schools must also teach responsibility to others.[11] This can only be done by providing the experience of interrelating with persons from dissimilar backgrounds and the experience of having others dependent on one's actions. In order to give youth the opportunities for interdependent activities directed toward collective goals, the Commission recommends that schools develop relationships with a host of programs and institutions that presently are not part of the formal instructional program.

The task for schools must be to break down the barriers to reality and spearhead the transition of the young into the adult world. A new national goal of educational policy must be to integrate youth into the community in functional roles that contribute materially to their maturation as adults.

Notes

1. Excerpted from a presentation by Willis W. Harman, commissioner, to the National Commission on Youth at Cornell University, Ithaca, N. Y., on May 11, 1977.
2. Harry S. Broudy, "Smoothing the Way From School to Society," in Ralph W. Tyler, ed., *From Youth to Constructive Adult Life: The Role of the Public School* (McCutchan Publishing Corporation, Berkeley, Calif., 1978), p. 16.
3. President's Science Advisory Committee, *Youth: Transition to Adulthood* (U.S. Government Printing Office, Washington, D.C., 1973), p. I-3.
4. Ibid., p. I-2.
5. Remarks made by Urie Bronfenbrenner, commissioner, to the National Commission on Youth at Cornell University, Ithaca, N.Y., on May 11, 1977 (transcribed).
6. James S. Coleman, *How Do the Young Become Adults?*, Center for Social Organization of Schools, Report no. 130 (Johns Hopkins University, Baltimore, Md., 1972), p. 5.
7. *Youth: Transition to Adulthood*, pp. S-3, S-4.
8. Ibid.
9. James S. Coleman, "Ways of Socialization," in Tyler, ed., *From Youth to Constructive Adult Life*, p. 40.
10. Ibid., pp. 41-42.
11. *Youth: Transition to Adulthood*, pp. I-4, I-5.

2
COMMUNITY-BASED
EDUCATION FOR YOUTH

Recommendation 2: Developing Community-Based Educational Programs. *Schools should develop imaginative, community-based programs in order to bring educational opportunities to youth on a dispersed, convenient basis. A future goal of all schools should be to make use of the community so that youth are allowed to function not as passive students but as active contributors to the community. The high schools in particular must play a coordinating role in the design and development of community-based programs. The intent is to break down the barriers that presently exist between the school and the community, thereby ensuring a better mix between youth and adults in the transitional process.*

Recommendation 3: Credit for Community-Based Education. *Secondary schools should award academic credit for successful learning experiences in those community-based programs that aid students in mastering basic knowledge areas and skills.*

Conventional wisdom has traditionally suggested that dropping out of high school was disastrous for the young. But what was true is becoming fallacious. A growing body of contemporary wisdom suggests that staying in school, as presently constituted, is equally disastrous for youth. Critics of public education maintain that schools impede countless numbers of youth who have potential from fulfilling their natural destiny as productive adults. This cacophony of voices has produced a common theme – education is too important to leave exclusively to the province of the schools.

Schools are graduating students who are unable to function in society. It has become increasingly evident that the secondary school is an incomplete context for development of many important facets of maturation. This factor, coupled with a lack of productive experiences in the real world, has made this a difficult period for older youth.

Schools need help. No longer can society rely exclusively on schools to carry out a task that is clearly a function of both the *school* and the *community*.

The history of American education reveals that in no sense have school and community become partners in a joint enterprise to educate the young. Instead, they operate as separate worlds, beholden to and controlled by independent institutional entities.[1]

At this point, one might ask how such obviously self-defeating practices have developed to fractionalize our society. To this issue the Commission gives its attention.

The Isolation of the School from the Community

When past errors continue to haunt us in the present, historical analysis is indispensable for understanding excesses and omissions. Such is the case of the present relationship between school and community. Only through its historical dimensions can a full measure of insight be gained into the present anachronistic relationship.

The writings of Charles Dickens on the exploitation of youth in an industrialized society dramatized the need to protect youth from the predatory practices of an evolving capitalistic system. American society responded to this need with a flurry of prescriptive legislation: the conditions under which child labor was permitted were strictly regulated, minimum wage rates were prescribed, and compulsory school laws were established.

The net result of such enactments was to extract the young from the marketplace and thrust them into school for increased periods of time. With every decade the length of formal schooling has expanded, steadily eroding the time that community-based activities once occupied, without substituting for them. The statutes and practices so necessary to protect youth in an earlier age in America currently serve a contrary purpose.[2] In many respects, they are the very factors that separate the school from the community. Instead of serving youth, the statutes do disservice to youth. Standing as barriers, they severely limit opportunities for youth to learn about work and the operations of the real world.

Schools as Holding Institutions

As schooling increasingly dominates the lives of youth, adolescence might be characterized as a longer "holding period." In addition to instructing youth in intellectual skills, schools also serve detentional or custodial purposes. Functioning as "holding tanks," schools excise youth from community life. Although we seldom acknowledge this function, the incarcerating role played by schools reflects societal ambivalence and general lack of clarity about the transition of youth to adult status.[3] As "holding tanks," however, schools perform useful services for adults. Youth are kept off the streets for lengthy periods during the day. Parents enjoy increased time for the pursuit of leisure. By keeping youth out of the job market, adults enjoy increased opportunity for employment.

Paul Goodman's haunting thesis in *Growing Up Absurd* is more meaningful today than it was a generation ago. It is hardly surprising that an extended period of ambiguity has become the standard rite of passage for the present generation of youth. Protected for longer periods in schools, students do not obtain the learning that is most vital to youth. As a consequence, Goodman argues, passivity is encouraged and stereotypes are reinforced.[4]

The Commission is unanimous in its belief that the "holding tank" syndrome be brought to an end as expeditiously as possible. It recommends strongly that immediate attention be given to decreasing the length of mandatory school attendance. A specific recommendation is that mandatory school attendance be lowered to age fourteen in every state. (This dramatic and controversial view is not included as a summary recommendation because it was set forth in detail in *The Reform of Secondary Education*, the 1973 report of the National Commission on the Reform of Secondary Education established by the Charles F. Kettering Foundation.)

Concomitant with this recommendation is one that would provide a number of viable work-study options in the community for those young people who choose to leave school at age fourteen. Such options should be considered part of an educational program, and they need to be developed in advance of, or in conjunction with, any lowering of the compulsory school age. Mere elimination of compulsory education after age fourteen offers no advantage to youth. Some specific examples of the community-based programs the Commission envisions will be analyzed later in this chapter.

Educational Consequences of Extended Schooling

To compensate for the excision of youth from the community, student roles have expanded to dominate the lives of the young. So large are its parameters in the lives of the young that the terms student and youth are used synonymously in the American vocabulary.

But here is the rub. The role of student is a passive one. It suffers from the "waiting game" syndrome – always in preparation for action, but never called to action in the world that exists outside the schoolhouse walls.

The consequences of an education that lacks an experiential dimension are enormous. John Dewey recognized this not long after the change occurred in historical fact, noting that the very worst form of instruction was that which "is not motivated and impregnated with a sense of reality by being intermingled with the realities of everyday life."[5]

In our complex society, one can be competent but not confident. Competence is necessary, but it is insufficient by itself. Rather, competence must be infused and suffused with confidence. Confidence is engendered from direct experience. Direct experience comes from community-based education.

The Commission does not claim to know the future. But it is already abundantly clear that the future demands a carefully planned approach involving youth in a variety of community-based settings in which youth can exercise increased initiative and responsibility.

As a step in this direction, the Commission recommends that a future goal for all schools be utilization of the community as an educational resource on a continuing basis. Community-based instruction affords youth opportunities to be contributors to and participants in the community as a part of an educational enterprise.

The isolation of the school from a community setting and the increased specialization of work have combined to separate youth from where the action is. Against this background of restraint one must ask: How do youth get a piece of the action? Where is it happening? What is the most appropriate locus for youth? It is in the community. Youth must be thrust into the community because this is where the action is happening. In the community arena the productive activities of a society take place.

Role of the Community

The roots of the problems surrounding the transition of youth to adulthood burrow deeply into the school and the community. The root structure is so complex and far-reaching that it exceeds the ameliorative competencies of any single institution. Only the community, acting in concert with the school, can provide the means necessary to make the transitional experience more effective for youth.

Presently many community institutions, beset with their conflicting responsibilities and allegiances, fail to see themselves as potential resources or active agents to assist youth. It is imperative that they do so. The substantial developmental resources of the community must become an integral part of an educational policy aiming at maximum development and utilization of youth potential. Accordingly, the Commission recommends that the resources of our major social, economic, and political institutions on the community level be incorporated into the high school curriculum to a greater degree than is the case at the present time.

Role of the School

Schools are where youth are. Thus, it is inescapable that schools play a key role in any program of community-based instruction. If participation by the community is essential, participation by the schools is crucial. Although schools and schooling in a formal setting are just one aspect of a community-based program, they constitute an integral link in the transitional process. A community-based instructional program does not in the least denigrate youth's needs for formal education. High schools must continue to instruct students in traditional skills and knowledge. The Commission does not lend its imprimatur to any of the proposals for abolishing schooling in a formal sense. Nor does the Commission subscribe to the idle rhetoric that places the schools beyond redemption.

It is highly doubtful that experiential, community-based education would by itself succeed without the basic literacy skills that the classroom teacher is trying to teach. The solution will depend on major change in the emphasis put on learning requirements.

The responsibility to learn must be placed on the student with the same force as the responsibility to teach is placed on the teacher. This can be done only if the consequences of not learning have immediate and direct consequences for the student. Without such a required reward and penalty system the improvement of education, whether classroom or experiential, is impossible. There is no magic in community-based instruction, experiential learning, or direct experience unless learning standards are understood and required.

The recommendations of the Commission imply a search for a more appropriate educational environment for youth, an environment that is more compatible with the real world. The focus of this quest centers on the following issue: What educational institutions are necessary and how can their instructional programs be best designed to respond to the needs of youth during the critical process of transition to adulthood?

Action-Learning: A New Locus for Youth

The Commission recommends strongly that high schools undertake a major effort to develop curricula that are *action-rich* in content rather than exclusively *knowledge-rich*. To accomplish this goal, the Commission considers it imperative that high schools become far more imaginative than they have been historically in arranging action-based educational opportunities for students on a dispersed and convenient basis.

Action-learning is defined by the Commission as learning from experience or associated study that is or would be accredited by an educational institution. In this locus, youth learn from work that may be undertaken part-time or full-time for a period of several months to several years. Action-learning has an element of novelty; it is not menial or repetitious. It is not classroom work; it takes place in the company of others in the community. It may involve guided study on the job in the form of internships or apprenticeships. Action-learning may be in paid jobs with private employers or in unpaid volunteer work with community service agencies.

Models of the types of action-learning envisioned by the Commission are already operational. Several programs deserve mention. In Syracuse, New York, for example, a number of neighboring school systems cooperate with Syracuse University in operating learning-resource centers where an impressive array of community organizations and individuals cooperate to provide action-rich instruction. Project ACT in Minneapolis, Minnesota, an experiment funded by the Danforth Foundation, is another example of action-learning. Secondary school students from six Minneapolis schools are engaged in volunteer service, internships, and community studies, and are shadowing workers in order to explore career options in a direct manner.

Action-learning assumes a variety of forms. From the myriad of existing programs, a common denominator is beginning to emerge. Increasingly, a community-based instructional setting is viewed as the most appropriate environment for coming to grips with the numerous issues that are grouped under the generic heading of transitional problems of youth.

The "brand name" of the projects varies. Regardless of the specific names and objectives of the projects, they are not mutually exclusive. In all of the projects, the following characteristics are evident:

> Youth learn by doing.
> Youth are offered a type of participation that gives them an opportunity to demonstrate responsible action.

Youth experience the consequences of their actions because such actions affect others.

Youth develop confidence to participate in the community as they master the requisite competencies for effective participation.

While recognizing that there is a certain degree of "definitional abstruseness" in a task of this nature, the many existing programs have been categorized into school programs, corporate programs, and service programs. This division provides an inkling of the various forces working on the community level to enhance the transitional process for youth.[6]

School Programs

High schools offer a wide variety of programs, mostly for occupational reasons, that place students in a community-based setting for at least part of their learning experiences.

Curriculum Education. Students design learning materials for other students. By these means students function as both creators and recipients of school curricula. In Enfield, Connecticut, students at Enfield High School wrote proposals, designed a prototype, and obtained funds for a social studies laboratory. Utilizing recording and visual equipment, students made documentaries on various problematic issues confronting both the town and themselves.

Instructional Education. By tutoring fellow students and younger children, participants enhance their own academic skills and gain personal satisfaction from helping others. Denton High School in Denton, Texas, has had five years of success with an elective course, Social Studies Lab, which involves high school students tutoring in the elementary school as part of a daily program.

Vocational Education. A major emphasis of schools' efforts to prepare youth for the world of work is in programs of a vocational nature. Approximately one-third of the nation's high school students are enrolled in these programs. In Dallas, Texas, the Skyline Center offers students a curriculum divided into twenty-seven different career clusters. Particular career clusters are determined by surveying the job market in the Dallas area and offering vocational courses in response to anticipated occupational needs.

Work-Study Education. Schools and outside agencies have developed a variety of programs that emphasize career awareness and development along with attempting to contribute to income maintenance for poor youth and prevent dropping out of school. In Maine, the Employment Security Commission recruited fifty-nine young people for a summer project. Some worked as counseling aides for young people. Others were employed as clerks in recreation, urban renewal, health, welfare, and law enforcement agencies. Participants were also offered language and social studies classes by instructors from the University of Maine.

Cooperative Education. Secondary schools combine school and work in planned programs of study. The high school and local businesses typically cooperate in a joint venture. The John Patterson High School in Dayton, Ohio, was the first public school to institute a formal cooperative education program for its students. It continues to offer an outstanding program in which educators and employers cooperate to provide youth on graduation with entry-level marketable skills.

Career Education. Career educators attempt to infuse career implications into the total school curriculum from kindergarten through twelfth grade. Emphasis is placed on practical applications of learning with reference to specific careers. In Mesa, Arizona, the schools have developed a Center for Career Development. Over 500 high school students participate in a program emphasizing field trips, guest speakers, guest lecturers, and taped interviews, along with work opportunities for students.

Alternative Education. A wide variety of options exists to extend the educational process into the community. In this setting community resources are utilized for various instructional purposes. In Philadelphia, Pennsylvania, the Parkway High School continues a pioneering effort to place students in community-based learning situations. Museums, hospitals, factories, and the like serve as a campus for learning experiences.

Corporate Programs

Employers offer a number of initiatives on both national and local levels. These efforts are largely job-oriented in nature. For the most part these programs are targeted at youth who have dropped out of school or who have graduated from school without marketable skills.

The National Alliance of Businessmen offers a variety of programs in urban centers aimed mainly at disadvantaged youth. The Youth Motivation Task Force puts disadvantaged youth into direct contact with a wide variety of successful businessmen who have had disadvantaged backgrounds themselves. Career Guidance Institutes have been established to improve the quality of job counseling offered to students by schools. The Guided Opportunities for Life Decisions program provides part-time jobs for disadvantaged high school students.

Teledyne Inc. has managed and operated Job Corps Centers since the Job Corps program began in 1965. These Teledyne centers are located in Phoenix, Arizona; Albuquerque, New Mexico; Pittsburgh, Pennsylvania; and Charleston, West Virginia. Since the program's inception, Teledyne has trained over 18,000 young people.

Service Programs

In addition to the initiatives of educators and employers, the service sector makes important contributions through various community-based programs.

Government-Sponsored Volunteer Programs. The federal government sponsors a number of programs, such as the Peace Corps and VISTA. Volunteers have completed at least high school and agree to join the program for a specified period of time. They serve as full-time volunteers.

School-Related Service Programs. These programs exist for youth still in high school. They are usually part-time and may or may not involve academic credit. They encompass a wide variety of programs and can be classified loosely along the following lines.

1. Helping others: In Hightstown, New Jersey, high school students participate in a youth-tutoring-youth program. They also tutor elementary school children, using remedial materials they have designed.
2. Service to the community: In New York City, Lower East Side students produce a community magazine, *The Fourth Street i.* The magazine is used as a voice for poor residents of various ethnic groups in the neighborhood.
3. Social action: In Manchester, New Hampshire, the West High School Ecology Club was formed to clean up the Merrimack River. The club also designs ecology lessons and teaches them to elementary school children, petitions for environmental legislation, and provides in-service programs in the construction and operation of environmental monitoring equipment.
4. Community internships: In Evergreen, Colorado, students in the alternate school program spend a half day a week interning with adults in the community, serving as apprentices to electricians, veterinarians, photographers, and store managers.
5. Executive internships: More than 7,000 students have interned under the auspices of the National Executive High School Internship Program, now operating in twenty-seven school

districts in seventeen states. This program, the largest of its kind, has interned high school students with judges, lawyers, government officials, teachers, and hospital administrators.

Community-Service Agencies. The voluntary sector provides important linkages between the business, labor, and educational establishments. The National Collaboration for Youth serves as an umbrella for twelve of the major youth organizations in the nation: the Boys' Clubs of America, the Girls Clubs of America, the Boy Scouts of America, the Girl Scouts of the U.S.A., the Camp Fire Girls, Future Homemakers of America, the National Board of the YWCAs, the National Board of the YMCAs, the National Federation of Settlements and Neighborhood Centers, the National Jewish Welfare Board, the 4-H, and the Red Cross Youth Service Programs. Almost 30 million young people between the ages of six and eighteen are enrolled in these organizations. They are assisted by more than 40,000 full-time professionals working with these various programs.

Anything that is not government funded or federally sanctioned tends to get overlooked. Yet, as can be seen through the following examples, these voluntary organizations form the backbone of community-based activities for youth. The Red Cross Youth Service Programs are involved in a new program called "Things You Never Learned in School." Young people in the plan are taught about personal budgeting, nutrition, credit, and consumer education. The Girls Clubs sponsors a program called "Jobs in the Future for You" (JIFFY). Girls are tested individually and given individual counseling, and their high school records are analyzed for proper placement. Additionally, they engage in role-playing for job interviews, study poise and dress techniques, fill out resumes, and visit state unemployment service centers. Finally, each girl is placed by the local club in a voluntary position that can be paid or unpaid. When a girl graduates from high school and leaves the club, she has a letter of recommendation and a resume that lists her high school work, her volunteer work at the club, and any other volunteer or extracurricular work. In Las Cruces, New Mexico, 4-H members created a business firm called Students Incorporated. The firm assumes legal liability for youth who are placed in a wide variety of jobs in the community ranging from park maintenance to mowing lawns and hauling trash. Last year over 800 youth were placed in jobs throughout the community and earned $109,000.

Government-Sponsored Youth Service Programs. As a result of recent legislation passed by the federal government, a number of federal programs are providing public service work opportunities for youth. Chapter 3 will deal at length with this aspect, examining the history of the movement along with analyzing the implications of a National Youth Service.

Community Involvement in Transitional Programs

In summary, perusal of the programs taking place on the grassroots level reveals a pragmatic response to the problems of youth. Communities across the nation are fashioning a wide range of responses to better meet the needs of high-school-age youth. Such variety is a direct reflection of the high level of local input into these programs. The Commission applauds this local initiative. Collectively, it constitutes the bedrock foundation so necessary to build a network of significant participatory experiences for youth.

The various programs illustrate clearly that resolution of the transitional problems of youth is better addressed at the local level rather than the state or national levels. What thrives in one community may not necessarily work in another community for a variety of reasons.

It is important that youth perceive community-based education as real work, important and necessary to the needs of the community. To this end the Commission recommends that high school students be granted academic credit for participatory experiences in the community. Whenever such experience is provided under the aegis of institutions other than the school, arrangements should be made for granting appropriate academic credit to participants. To preserve the integrity of the credits granted, careful monitoring must be built into every program.

In order to keep the purposes of schooling clear in the minds of all concerned, academic credit should be given only for what is learned in school or for its clear equivalents. This distinction is essential to the improvement of the learning process and learning the basic skills. Giving credit for experience outside the school too easily becomes an excuse for not learning the basic skills. Confusion about what is to be learned in school has weakened the school in one of its most important capacities – the capacity to train the mind.

Implicit in this confusion of academic and nonacademic work is the presumption that time spent in the classroom is wasted. It is not wasted if basic skill and knowledge goals are being achieved. If they are not being achieved, it is doubtful that they will be achieved elsewhere.

Giving academic credit for successful learning experiences in community-based programs depends on what that experience is. If that experience aids students in learning how to read, write, and do basic computation, or in mastering basic knowledge areas, academic credit would seem appropriate. If, on the other hand, the experience does not do this, giving academic credit would subvert the purpose and the results of schooling. Nothing is to be gained from giving academic credit for experience that makes no demands on the learning capacity of the individual. Therefore, great care should be taken to define the nature of community experience for which academic credit is given.

The Commission recognizes that funding for community-based programs is likely to come from state and federal agencies. However, it is imperative that program design should rest ultimately with local initiative. Accordingly, the Commission recommends that funding for local participatory programs should be as much as possible on a "no strings attached" basis. The federal and state roles should be limited to providing program visibility, funding support, and program monitoring.

Finally, it is apparent to the Commission that schools by themselves cannot provide adequate community-based educational programs. Nor is it desirable that they attempt unilaterally to add this dimension to their instructional programs. Rather, schools, employers, service organizations, labor leaders, government agencies, and others must participate in a cooperative effort to ensure effective transitional programs. It is still unclear at this point how best to facilitate and encourage such efforts. There is a clear need, however, to involve a wide range of community institutions and constituencies in collaborative planning efforts. In Chapter 4 youth transitional planning councils are proposed as the means to accomplish this end.

Toward Community-Based Instruction

The Commission defines *community-based education* as the means to give youth a sense of membership in the community through a variety of productive action-rich experiences. This definition can be fleshed out by contrasting it with classroom-based approaches. Community-based instruction often makes classroom-based instruction more effective, as in the following examples:

> Youth may transfer the knowledge gained from classroom instruction to real-life situations.
> Critical thinking skills or problem-solving techniques learned

in the classroom can be utilized to resolve community problems.

Concepts and generalizations learned in the classroom can be enriched and enlivened by reference to similar examples on the community level.

Data can be gathered from the community about a persisting problem or issue that has been studied in the classroom. Then hypotheses and generalizations can be developed from this data bank.

Problems and pressing issues presented from textbooks in a classroom setting can be raised to a new level of consciousness by observing similar problems and issues in a local community setting.

In addition to enhancing classroom instruction, community-based education can open new vistas for youth. Some of the following opportunities can be experienced by youth in a community setting:

Performing tasks that are mutually rewarding to the community at large and the individual actor

Developing an increased measure of responsibility by making logistical decisions about how to proceed most effectively on a task or project

Having others dependent on one's actions

Developing a feeling of confidence arising from mastery of a problem or task

Experiencing the sense of camaraderie or civic pride arising from the efforts of many individuals to accomplish a particular task or achieve a desired goal

Developing a more balanced mix of adults with young persons in community-based environments

Equally important, community-based education adds a caring dimension to the curriculum. Youth interact with the community on a direct and personalized basis. The community serves as an object of study, as an instructional setting, and, most of all, as a source of people who have important skills and knowledge to impart. In all these ways, the natural warmth and concern of community members for their young serve to minimize the period of transitional journey to adulthood.

In this environment, youth do not learn about others who care.

They participate in care. They assume responsibility for and to other human beings beyond the school walls. Through the community then, youth learn how caring is done, what it means, and how difficult but rewarding it is.

A Final Note

A few caveats are in order at this point. The history of curriculum design is replete with catchy slogans, glossy curriculum packages, instructional practices that capture the imagination, impressive statistical data, eloquent testimonials, and so on. All such things are superfluous, however, if they cannot be translated into viable programs. Too often, impressive programs are mere paper monuments. Oftentimes curriculum planners choose to ignore or do not foresee obstacles that hinder or prevent implementation.

Skepticism of this nature is well founded. The Commission is acutely aware that the curricular change it envisions is a formidable task, and would still be formidable even in a climate more receptive to educational innovation. Efforts to integrate community-based learning into existing curricular programs are likely to be confronted by a host of obstacles. Among the more salient are the following:

Traditional beliefs pertaining to the custodial function of the schools

Skepticism of parents, students, and educators about the programs

Rigid curriculum requirements established either through local expression or by state fiat

Logistical issues surrounding the transportation of students into the community

Financial arrangements over liability for students out of school and on job locations

Inflexible scheduling practices

Minimum wage requirements for full-time paid positions

Union rules or contractual arrangements for specific occupational settings

Credentialing or accrediting practices of trade organizations, in cooperation with state agencies, that delay or restrict entry into such occupations as those of barber, beautician, chauffeur, and day-care aide

Sexual stereotypes that preclude youth from positions as secretaries and mechanics

Such obstacles are the more visible features of the barriers to change erected by various institutions and constituencies "to protect their turf." Some organizations reflect either insensitivity or unwillingness to respond to the needs of their clients, while others, it must be recognized, are simply incapable of response to changing demands.

All this does not downgrade the necessity for community-based education. Instead, it further compels one to break down the barriers separating the school from the community.

It must be recognized that no single instructional program can remedy all the problems faced by youth today. There is strength in a diversity of approaches. As we have painstakingly become aware in recent years with the example of the school system, no single institution or approach is sufficient as the major environment for socialization to adulthood.

Community-based education, however, impels and enables youth to educate themselves in a manner uniquely appropriate to their particular needs, interests, and circumstances. They can try various occupations by design and choice rather than by chance or mistake. This much-needed flexibility leads to informed decision making as youth approach adulthood.

Notes

1. Willard Wirtz et al., *The Boundless Resource: A Prospectus for an Education-Work Policy* (New Republic Book Company, Washington, D.C., 1975), p. 1.

2. Ralph W. Tyler, "Tomorrow's Education," *American Education*, August-September 1975, p. 17.

3. James P. Shaver and William Strong, *Facing Value Decisions: Rationale-Building for Teachers* (Wadsworth Publishing Company, Belmont, Calif., 1976), pp. 148-149.

4. Paul Goodman, *Growing Up Absurd* (Random House, New York, N.Y., 1956), p. 217.

5. John Dewey, *Democracy and Education* (Macmillan Publishing Company, New York, N.Y., 1966), p. 163.

6. An excellent source of information on programs for improving the transition from school to work is the National Commission for Manpower Policy, *From School to Work: Improving the Transition* (U.S. Government Printing Office, Washington, D.C., 1976).

For information on the volunteer movement see National Child Labor Committee, *Youth Serving the Community: Realistic Public Service Roles for Young Workers*, Final Report no. 21-36-77-12 (Employment and Training Administration, U.S. Department of Labor, 1978).

The volunteer service movement at the secondary level is outlined in a number of publications of ACTION, *National Student Volunteer Program: High School Student Volunteers; High School Courses With Volunteer Components.* Also see *Synergist* 2:2 (fall 1973).

Also see the National Commission on Resources for Youth's excellent survey of experiential roles for youth in a wide range of settings. *New Roles for Youth in the School and Community* (Citation Press, New York, N.Y., 1974).

3

NATIONAL SERVICE FOR YOUTH

Recommendation 4: Creation of a National Youth Service. *The Congress of the United States should establish a National Youth Service guaranteeing all American youth the opportunity for at least one year of full-time service to their community or to the nation.*

All youth, male and female alike, between the ages of sixteen and twenty-one should be guaranteed the opportunity to participate for at least one year of full-time service in the program; all youth between the ages of fourteen and twenty-one would be eligible for part-time participation in National Youth Service programs as part of school-related cooperative programs. Part-time service would be rendered in one's own community; full-time participation would most likely entail service in distant locations.

Recommendation 5: Mandatory Registration for National Youth Service. *Congress should enact legislation requiring all American citizens, both male and female, at the age of eighteen to register for the opportunity to participate in a National Youth Service program. Mandatory registration will assure that all eighteen-year-olds receive counseling and guidance in relation to National Youth Service opportunities and values.*

Youth transitional planning councils should be designated as the mechanism through which compulsory registration is accomplished. In the event that there is no youth transitional planning council operating on the local level, registration of participants should take place through the local Selective Service office.

Recommendation 6: Advocating National Youth Service Experience as a Condition of Employment. *All employers—individuals, agencies, institutions, and businesses—should encourage youth to register and participate in the National Youth Service experience. Employers should advocate at least one year of service experience as a prerequisite for employment.*

Recommendation 7: Educational Entitlements. *Serious consideration should be given to incorporating an educational entitlement voucher—a type of GI Bill of Rights for service — into any plan for National Youth Service. Opportunity vouchers should grant one year of educational entitlement for each year of service experience up to a maximum of four years.*

"And so, my fellow Americans, ask not what your country can do for you; ask what you can do for your country."

Responding to President John F. Kennedy's challenge, youthful legions flocked to serve with their hands and minds in projects at home and around the world. A crusade of youth marched out of Washington, D.C., determined to eliminate need and injustice.

But Camelot faded as quickly as it had blossomed. The muffled drumbeat of November 1963 was soon raised to a more strident tempo. Instead of waging war on poverty, ignorance, and human frailty, young people marched off to protest the war in Vietnam. For the protestors, this was the 1960s version of making the world safe for democracy. Rejection and riot replaced sacrifice and service as the marching orders of the day.

The call to serve is being raised once again. It is sustained by a diverse coalition — Democrats and Republicans, liberals and conservatives — calling for Congress to compel all eighteen-year-old youth to serve either in a military or a civilian capacity for at least one year. This time, however, the call to serve is not for all the right reasons. Unemployment among youth and military manpower needs have thrust National Youth Service into the limelight again.

The Need for National Youth Service

Actually, the need for National Youth Service runs much deeper than the current travail. Inherent problems exist with a socialization process that mandates the placement of youth in holding institutions where waiting becomes the central task in life. At the very stage in human growth and development when energy and idealism are at their peak, there is scant opportunity for youth to make any kind of contribution to society, to experience the challenge of completing a task commensurate with one's abilities and interests, to feel the satisfaction gained from completing a task creditably, to feel the joy and endure the pain of participating in the arena of the real world, to act instead of wait.[1]

If service programs did nothing more than fulfill the need of youth to be recognized as contributing members of the community, that would justify their existence. But there is hope for more. Youth can make an immediate contribution to the welfare of the communities of which they are members. Youth are not just a resource for the future; they are citizens who can contribute to build a better society today.[2]

Without question, there is immediate need for such a massive infusion of youth power. Providing opportunities for constructive service by youth can have a dual effect: such youth power can contribute materially to the community while also harnessing and nurturing the idealism of the young.

Several studies have demonstrated a clear need to utilize youth power in more constructive ways. A 1965 study by the Office of Economic Opportunity estimated a need for 4,300,000 persons of minimum skills and educational background. A year later, the National Commission on Technology, Automation and Economic Progress estimated the need at 5,300,000 persons.[3]

More recently, the Agriculture Department indicated that in 1975 it could provide 40,000 man-years of employment per year for skilled and unskilled labor. The Forest Service stated its needs for 260,000 man-years in order to complete needed conservation projects. At the same time, the Department of the Interior estimated that a variety of conservation projects would consume 90,000 man-years of labor.[4]

Clearly then, in analyzing both the defined needs and the available resources, there is more than ample potential for youth to accomplish these needed tasks through service to the nation.

A Working Definition of National Youth Service

The National Commission on Youth defines *National Youth Service* as the guarantee to all young men and women of the opportunity to engage in a period of full-time or part-time community service or service on environmental projects. It embraces the belief that an opportunity should be given to each young person to serve the country in a manner consistent with national needs and his or her own educational background and interests.

Service learning gives participants an opportunity to share the talents and the learning that they have already acquired with others, while simultaneously learning new skills and performing a useful service. The length of service varies according to the nature of the placement and the interests of the participants. In any case, however, it is never a permanent placement.

Both academic credit and monetary credit is granted for service. The precise amount of credit is determined on the basis of the amount of time devoted by the participant to the program, coupled with evaluations of the service experience. Evaluations are made by the participant, by the sponsoring agency, and by the educational officer attached to the project.

Historical Antecedents for National Youth Service

A deeper understanding of the concept of National Youth Service is gained by analyzing the historical origins of the concept.

National Youth Service Under FDR

Crisis was the catalyst for the initial efforts to establish a National Youth Service. Both the Civilian Conservation Corps (CCC) and the National Youth Administration (NYA) were significant aspects of President Franklin D. Roosevelt's legislative program. One of FDR's first actions during the "100 Days" was the establishment of the Civilian Conservation Corps. This was year one for the concept of National Youth Service. By July 4, 1933, three months after the formation of the CCC was announced, 250,000 young men were enrolled in various forest and park camps across the nation. Peak enrollment reached approximately 500,000 young men by 1935. From 1933 until its termination in 1943, the CCC provided useful conservation work and needed financial assistance for nearly 3 million young men. Voluntarism had come of age.

So successful was the CCC as a vehicle for ameliorating the debilitating effects of the Depression on young men that it even received enthusiastic endorsement from Alfred Landon, Roosevelt's presidential rival in 1936. Undoubtedly a major reason for this universal acclaim was its ubiquitous impact. Reforestation projects, hiking trails, and vacation cabins, along with ponds and lakes, were all highly visible and could be utilized by all for enjoyment. This point needs to be underscored. It is especially relevant for present service proposals since many of the service projects envisioned offer considerably less visibility. Tutoring a child or being a companion to a nursing home resident bears results seen by a much smaller clientele.[5]

If the CCC was Franklin Roosevelt's progeny, the National Youth Administration was Eleanor Roosevelt's baby. It troubled Mrs. Roosevelt that the CCC was administered by the army. Moreover, she sought a much broader approach to national service for youth, one that would harness the energies and idealism of the young for national purposes. Aware that the problem of youth unemployment was of a structural rather than cyclical nature, she pondered: "Now what are you going to say to our youth who are not wanted in industry? We have no plans for you! We offer you nothing, we simply restrict your activities . . . I would like to see us institute a volunteer service to the country open to both boys and girls."[6] Thus the NYA was born.

When the National Youth Administration was created in 1935, it was one of many progressive projects given impetus by the New Deal. It enrolled both men and women, sixteen to twenty-four years old, and it had programs both for students and nonstudents.[7] Significantly, when signing the NYA into law, FDR stated: "I have determined that we shall do something for the nation's unemployed youth because we can ill-afford to lose the skill and energy of these young men and women. I want the youth of America to have something to say about what is being done for them. They must have their chance in school, their turn as apprentices, and their opportunity for jobs—a chance to work and earn for themselves."[8]

Over the life span of the NYA, from 1935 to 1943, nearly five million young people worked in their hometowns building roads and streets, serving in nursery schools, and filling jobs in government agencies. The country flirted briefly with the idea of institutionalizing a full-fledged National Youth Service on a permanent basis in 1941. A young representative from the Texas hill country, himself a former supervisor in the NYA, introduced a bill to this effect. Fate would have it that when Congressman Lyndon Johnson proposed a merger of the National Youth Administration with the Civilian Conservation Corps, the month was December 1941. Fifteen million men went off to war following the attack on Pearl Harbor. The youth problem was shelved for years to come.

Post–World War II Developments

In the decades following 1945, the concept of national service for youth has taken on entirely new dimensions. Initially, it was considered as a viable way to demonstrate our commitment to the newly achieved peace; then it was considered as an alternative to conscription; finally, it was viewed as a means of enabling students to acquire relevant educational experience. Presently, it is viewed by many as the most expedient means to solve the vexing problem of unemployment among youth.

While neither so exciting nor so massive as the New Deal experiments, several of the youth programs that have emerged relating to the National Youth Service concept warrant brief mention. Collectively, the programs provide some guidelines for a National Youth Service. They include the following:

Mobilization of youth
Educational implications of service learning
Idealism of youth
Targeted programs for youth
Magnitude of the need for youth service
Ability of youth to perform needed service[9]

GI Bill of Rights

It is widely acknowledged that the GI Bill of Rights is one of the most worthwhile and substantial investments that the United States has ever made in its young people. Its economic feasibility is unchallenged. Best estimates calculate that in terms of increased federal tax payments from 1946 to 1973, the GI bill yielded a sixteenfold return on a $15 billion investment.[10]

An additional outcome of the GI bill that defied predictions was that the educational interlude many young people were forced to take proved to be neither detrimental nor threatening to the American educational system.[11]

Peace Corps

Established by President Kennedy in 1961, the Peace Corps plowed new ground, illustrating government trust in the young along with a willingness to place youth in challenging and responsible positions. Perhaps even more valuable than the services provided by the corps to other nations are the personal educational experiences derived by the participants. The lesson to be drawn from this experience is that when trusted and given responsible positions, young people respond in kind.

In 1967 the Peace Corps operated on a budget of $100 million with a peak enrollment of 15,000 persons. Presently it enrolls approximately 7,000 corpsmen and operates on an $80 million budget.

Job Corps and Neighborhood Youth Corps

As part of Lyndon Johnson's Great Society programs, the Job Corps and Neighborhood Youth Corps were created in 1963 to wage a war on poverty. By legislative mandate, both programs aim to serve those labeled as "economically disadvantaged" by federally specified poverty guidelines.

Currently approximately 430,000 sixteen- to twenty-one-year-olds per year are enrolled in the Job Corps at a cost of $6,500 per man-year. Its purpose is to assist young people who need and can benefit from intensive programs of educational and vocational training along with complementary services while residing in residential centers. Although the dropout rate from the program hovers near 50 percent, the job placement rate of those who remain in the program is an impressive 90 percent.

One of several manpower programs decategorized by the Comprehensive Employment and Training Act (CETA) of 1973 was the Neighborhood Youth Corps. In its present reduced capacity, it continues to serve nearly one million youth from the ages of fourteen to twenty-two in summer employment. In recent years the program has come under fire for providing only "dead-end" jobs and for "make-work" projects that fail to contribute to the educational development of youth. The annual budget is approximately $750,000.

Both the Job Corps and the Neighborhood Youth Corps provide useful insights into future program development. Both lack many of the essential components for a successful National Youth Service program. Essentially, they are relief programs aimed at the poor, the dropout, and the misplaced. In addition, they fail to provide the inspirational setting so necessary for a successful community service program.

VISTA

Volunteers in Service to America (VISTA) is a national service program envisaged as a domestic Peace Corps. The program seeks to involve persons over the age of eighteen who possess qualifications commensurate to those individuals recruited by the Peace Corps. Thus, like the Peace Corps, VISTA tends to be elitist in composition. The volunteers work in poverty-related areas. In its twelve-year existence, the program has deviated little from its original mandate. VISTA's current budget of $25 million supports approximately 4,500 volunteers, half of whom are between the ages of eighteen and twenty-four.

College Work-Study Program

The original intent of the federally funded College Work-Study Program was to help needy students work their way through college by involving them in the antipoverty movement. The government pays 80 percent of the wages paid to students while the college contributes the remainder. Unfortunately, the colleges have converted the program into a massive sinecure, maintaining most of the jobs on campus, thereby perverting the original objective of the program.

Urban Corps

With the aid of federal funds, approximately seventy Urban Corps programs have been funded across the nation. Based on the successful program instituted in 1966 in New York City, city agencies provide summer employment for thousands of college students.

Youth Conservation Corps

In 1971, the Department of the Interior announced the creation of the small but highly visible Youth Conservation Corps (YCC). Under the direction of the Departments of the Interior and Agriculture, it provides a cross-section of fifteen- to eighteen-year-old youth with summer employment in environmentally related jobs. About 33 percent of the youth are disadvantaged; about 60 percent are from middle-income families of all racial groups; the remainder are from upper-income families. Both sexes are equally represented. The purpose is to assist existent conservation agencies by completing projects that will conserve, preserve, maintain, and enhance public lands and waters. The 1978 appropriation authorization is $60 million, providing summer jobs for 47,000 youth. Money is passed on to the states in the form of grants for conservation projects; 80 percent of the grant money is federal, with the states providing the remaining 20 percent either in kind or in cash.

In its seven years of existence, from a cost-benefit ratio, the YCC program has returned at least 78¢ on every federal dollar through the work of youth in the various sponsoring agencies.[12]

National Youth Service Experiments by ACTION

Of major note is a prototype National Youth Service (NYS) experiment launched by the ACTION agency in Washington state in 1973. If the outcomes of this small pilot program are indicative of the experiences one might anticipate from a full-scale program, the future prospect of NYS looks good.

All young people in the greater-Seattle area, ages eighteen to twenty-five, were invited to enroll in a year of community service. Unlike the elitist Peace Corps and VISTA programs, the *Program for Local Service* (PLS) was open to all. Less than two months after the program commenced, 1,600 applicants applied for 1,200 job listings. Participating sponsors contributed $150 per man-year to the program.

Unlike other service programs outlined, applicants were not placed in positions. With the help and guidance of facilitators called brokers or matchmakers, potential enrollees were acquainted with jobs that matched their abilities and interests, and interviews were arranged with several cooperating sponsors.

The ACTION agency monitored and evaluated the Program for Local Service, but paychecks were dispersed to youth through sponsors. Approximately 60 percent of the enrollees were women; the minority participation rate of 20 percent was over double the minority rate for the Seattle area. Volunteers had a slightly better than average education but were distinctly poorer. Most significantly, seven out of ten volunteers were unemployed and actively looking for work.

The outcomes are highly significant in any consideration of National Youth Service. The value of the services performed was judged to be double the amount of monies invested in the program. When surveyed six months after leaving the service, only 18 percent (compared to an entry-level figure of 70 percent) were unemployed and looking for work. Most importantly, the majority of participants rated the PLS program valuable in influencing their future.[13]

Finally, the program demonstrated the viability of a system of local service delivery, training, programming, and supervision. Local reaction to the program has been so positive that in June 1977 Governor Dixy Lee Ray signed into law a bill unanimously passed by both houses of the Washington legislature calling for expansion of the program statewide. Now that ACTION has discontinued funding of the experimental PLS program, funding has been taken over largely from the Comprehensive Employment and Training Act.[14]

Similar conclusions were reached in the small ACTION-sponsored program, *University Year for Action.* This program, which essentially emulates VISTA, is administered by local colleges that carry out all aspects of the program—recruitment, training, placement, programming, and supervision.[15]

YEDPA

As the Carter administration took office in January 1977, the deteriorating plight of American youth inspired a flurry of legislation. Over a dozen bills were introduced in the first session of the 95th Congress pertaining to youth service and employment. Responding to the initiative, President Jimmy Carter signed into law on August 5, 1977, the Youth Employment and Demonstration Projects Act (YEDPA). If fully implemented and funded on a continuing basis, the Act has the potential to become landmark legislation in the National Youth Service movement. Collectively, its provisions constitute far more than a simple expansion of previous legislative programs.[16]

YEDPA places significant emphasis on community service and service-learning. Careful analysis of the act reveals that over 90 percent of the work done by youth would be similar to that done in a National Youth Service program.[17]

The billion-dollar measure contains a number of provisions that may serve as testing grounds for launching a National Youth Service program. The following projects have been funded since the act was signed into law.[18]

- $233.3 million has been allotted for the creation of the Young Adult Conservation Corps (YACC). Patterned along the lines of the CCC, it is open to all unemployed youth between the ages of sixteen and twenty-three.
- $109 million has been authorized for Youth Incentive Entitlement Projects, which guarantee jobs to poor sixteen- to nineteen-year-olds who agree to complete their high school studies. (This constitutes the largest social experiment in our nation's history.)[19]
- $115 million has been granted to the Youth Community Conservation and Improvement Project. A public-works-type program, it is open to unemployed youth sixteen to nineteen with preference given to poor and disadvantaged youth.
- $8 million in funding was appropriated for a Youth Employment Training Program for youth employment projects linked to community development corporations selected by the Department of Housing and Urban Development (HUD).

A final provision of YEDPA is highly significant. Eight million dollars was provided for a national service test in Syracuse, New York. The project, known as *Youth Community Service*, began operating in March 1978 under the direction of ACTION. In many respects it is based on the experience of the successful PLS program in Washington.

A Viable Legacy

To sum up, the nation has had, in balance, nearly a half century of good experience with proto–National Youth Service programs. As a result, a sound foundation has been established for national service. The rich and positive legacy generated by programs ranging from the original CCC project to Seattle's Program for Local Service enhances the prospect for future efforts of this nature.

The cumulative effects of the national service experience are both interesting and significant. Each generation of planners has benefited from the efforts of the past. With this has come the realization that a viable program entails more than simply picking up and dusting off past models. While general operating principles may remain the same, any new program for National Youth Service requires additional fine tuning to meet the needs of present-day youth.

Community perceptions and past efforts are particularly revealing. Service programs based on the original CCC model have been endorsed heartily by Americans for nearly fifty years. No other government program has merited such consistent acclaim. In part at least, this must be attributed not only to the participants' personal development but also to the degree that the labor performed in the program visibly enhanced the life of the community.

Most importantly, the programs have clearly demonstrated that conceptually and programmatically a National Youth Service is a viable option for the present. Unquestionably, it merits serious consideration as a means to assist and enhance the transitional process of youth.

Some Present Supportive Trends
for National Youth Service

Along with the strong impulses from the past, a number of compelling circumstances in the present support a National Youth Service. In fact, it might be argued that this is precisely why we have failed to enact an ongoing program. Government programs, like humans, invariably suffer when they are the object of either too much or too little prescriptive effort.

No further argument need be made regarding the economic reasons for National Youth Service. In fact, a good deal of the current reasoning has been voiced over much of the past two decades. All of our recent presidents have, in favoring such a program, frequently cited economics.

Since the report of the Scranton Commission on Campus Unrest recommended national service as a way of providing relevant education for youth, such service has also been accepted without serious opposition as a viable educational alternative.

Another factor receiving increased attention involves the service dimension of the program. As pointed out earlier in this chapter, latest estimates project a need for at least 4 million youth to perform much-needed conservation work and community service.

Finally, since the turn of the century, simultaneous with the isolation of youth in the schools, there have been psychological reasons that argue for national service for the young. For much of this century, individuals have expressed the idea of giving youth the chance to prove themselves. It was William James who best expressed this atavistic quality in his 1906 appeal, "The Moral Equivalent of War":

> To coal and iron mines, to freight trains, to fishing fleets in December, to dish-washing, clothes-washing, and window-washing, to road-building and tunnel-making, to foundries and stokeholes, and to the frames of skyscrapers, would our gilded youths be drafted off, according to their choice, to get the childishness knocked out of them and to come back into society with healthier sympathies and soberer ideas. They would have paid their blood-tax, done their own part in the immemorial human warfare against nature; they would tread the earth more proudly, the women would value them more highly, they would be better fathers and teachers of the following generation.

Arguing on the basis of James's observations, it would seem reasonable that an experience of this nature would give rise to a modest leavening effect, and thereby contribute, in small measure at least, to a greater democratization of society.

A Call for a National Youth Service

For all of the above reasons then, the National Commission on Youth believes that National Youth Service is an idea whose time has come. In this spirit, the Commission recommends unanimously and calls on the Congress of the United States to establish a National Youth Service as testimony of the nation's commitment to its youth. Developed to its fullest dimensions, a National Youth Service possesses the potential to serve youth as a sorely needed rite of passage in the transition to adulthood.

Some Vexing Issues of National Youth Service

The issues surrounding a program of National Youth Service are numerous and complex. Despite voluminous amounts of dialogue and writing, there is slight evidence of closure on many of these issues. If a National Youth Service is to become a reality, however, such vexing issues can neither be evaded nor ignored.

For purposes of analysis, the issues are considered as separate entities. In reality, most of the issues are closely intertwined. Many are controversial in nature. A major portion of the Commission's deliberations was devoted to analyzing and thrashing out the ramifications of these issues. Discussion was far-ranging; expert testimony was elicited from many sources; spirited exchanges among the Commissioners was not infrequent; and unanimity was not achieved or expected on every issue. The recommendations that emerge from these deliberations attempt to strike a delicate balance on these vexing problems.

Membership. If a situation existed whereby the nation was largely unsympathetic to the concept of national service for youth or in the event an administration unenlightened about the problems of youth held office, a strong case could still be made for targeting specific kinds of youth for the program. Similarly, in the event that the youth resources of the nation were scarce in number, then it would be necessary to establish minimal quotas to make the program operational.

Neither of these conditions exists. Thus, the Commission rejects targeting membership for a service program, coming down instead on the side of universalism.

Youth resources in the older age groups (sixteen to twenty-one) exist in such abundant numbers that if a program for National Youth Service is targeted in any manner a stigmatizing effect will result. A useful example of this phenomenon is gained by comparing the Neighborhood Youth Corps Program with the recent Program for Local Service in Washington state. In the former, a targeted program for poor youth, a pejorative connotation developed early. The program was stigmatized merely as a handout to alleviate the misery of poverty and as having few, if any, redeeming features. By comparison, the PLS program, which was not targeted, has not developed a negative image.

If participants in an NYS are given a choice of job opportunities, their choices will inevitably reflect their personal educational attainments as well as their vocational aspirations. Consequently, the elitism that is associated with the Peace Corps and VISTA programs may very well develop in an NYS, albeit to a lesser degree.

Ideally, NYS would be available for participation by all youth. However, in a situation of economic constraints, it may be necessary to channel a substantial proportion of financial resources to those youth who are most in need. This is a very fuzzy situation. All young Americans need work experience, job training, and opportunities for meaningful positive involvement in their society. Thus, there is a very delicate balance that must be struck between not wanting a targeted program for the poor and not wanting a program that is quickly snapped up by a powerful middle-class constituency as a symbol of elite status.

The Commission recommends that all youth, male and female alike, between the ages of sixteen and twenty-one be guaranteed the opportunity for at least one year of full-time service in NYS; all youth between the ages of fourteen and twenty-one would be eligible for part-time participation in NYS programs as part of a school-related cooperative program.

Nature of the Service Experience. What type of experience will both enable youth to escape the stigmatization of make-work programs and at the same time meet their individual needs?

The experience of some of the Great Society youth programs, such as the Neighborhood Youth Corps, has demonstrated clearly the negative effects that can accrue from federally sponsored make-work programs. On one hand, there is something to be said for programs that provide a controlled environment for those youth who are not ready for adult-level responsibilities. On the other hand, if programs do not strive to provide legitimate work experience to youth, they will inevitably reach a point where they are characterized as make-work or emergency relief measures.

Nothing would be more inimical to the concept of National Youth Service than to have the program perceived as a dole or handout to youth. Nothing would poison middle-class attitudes toward NYS more effectively. If this were to happen, it would curtail any chance for broad-based participation by youth.

Such a turn of events would be analogous to the fate of vocational education. At the turn of the century, the concept of vocational education, that all people be educated for a job, was a lofty ideal embraced by all citizens. In time, because of the numerous deficiencies in the program, it was perceived by middle-class Americans as learning about work in a body shop or in a kitchen. As a result, the middle class rejected it as an educational alternative for their children.

A realistic way of escaping stigmatization for a program of NYS is to build a wide range of productive activities – education, service, and work – into a comprehensive program that would be available and attractive to all eligible youth. Above all, incentives must be provided to participants to spur them into these various types of experiences. This implies that any program of NYS must go well beyond the monolithic goals of the New Deal initiatives. The program must attach a high value to a wide diversity of experiences and alternatives to make the program infinitely more attractive and comprehensive than merely providing jobs.

The Commission recommends that any program of NYS provide comprehensive opportunities for the participants to acquire work experience and training, to contribute service to the community, and to obtain educational experience.

Educational Linkages. The issue of formal education must also be addressed. One of the major, but largely unnoticed, shortcomings of the early New Deal programs was the extreme variability that existed in the educational dimensions of the programs. Although the educational component was supposed to be an integral part of the CCC experience, in fact it varied drastically.

A program of National Youth Service cannot exist in a vacuum. To be successful, it must interact with a variety of institutions, including secondary schools, vocational schools, and colleges.

The relationship between NYS and secondary schools deserves especial attention because the level of interaction would be immediate and direct. Those secondary schools that have developed the most imaginative and far-reaching community-based educational programs would be the first to feel the effects of an NYS. Competition would ensue between NYS programs and secondary schools, both attempting to draw youth from, and operate programs on, the same community base. More significantly, NYS programs might begin to engulf and inhibit alternative, service, and vocational educational programs offered by the schools. Ultimately, this would lead to a redefinition of secondary education if the school were restricted to offering only the traditional academic pursuits.[20]

While the curtailment of some of the instructional functions of the secondary schools may not be all bad, it is doubtful that secondary school educators would allow this to happen without prolonged and acrimonious debate. Similarly, it is doubtful that without support from the secondary schools, NYS will be a successful program. In summary, the educational dimension of NYS is still clouded. Thus, it is necessary to survey the variety of linkages that can be developed between NYS and secondary schools and determine what kinds of relationships are most desirable.

The Commission foresees vast potential for the development of many educative elements and components under NYS. Several major decisions will have to be made by local community sponsors. First, it will be necessary to determine the role NYS will play in the community. It might be decided to use NYS exclusively in the area of conservation. In any case, the specific service areas must be delineated. Next, it will be necessary to decide how and to what extent the schools should be involved with programs offered by NYS.

There are a number of possible forms that this program could assume. For instance, a student might go to school mornings and spend afternoons working in an NYS program or go to school three to four days per week and spend the remaining two days in the program. Another option might be going to school for a designated period of weeks and working in an NYS program for a similar period in alternating fashion. Finally, secondary school students might work in an NYS program for an entire school quarter or semester. In each instance, the student would be granted an appropriate amount of credit for NYS work.

Other possibilities include having students work after school, receiving supervision from the local NYS sponsor and participating in a program with no connection to the school system. However, as the major youth-serving institution of the nation, secondary schools can quite appropriately become involved in such a program.

The city of Baltimore, Maryland, has utilized this concept in a creative program called Harbor City Learning. This CETA-sponsored program, jointly administered by the Mayor's Office of Manpower Services and the Board of Education, involves 1,600 youth in a variety of activities. Youth alternate between going to school for two weeks and working for two weeks in service functions. The school system provides a principal, assistant principals, and a score of teachers, while the mayor's office supplies youth coordinators, counselors, and support staff.

The lesson to be drawn from this example is that it is feasible for two separate institutional entities to work together, to pool resources, and to create an effective, operational youth service program.

As well as providing services and programs for youth, secondary schools could benefit directly from the services of NYS volunteers in their educational programs. Specifically, participants could serve as tutors or teachers' aides. High school graduates might serve as teachers' aides on both elementary and secondary levels, performing a variety of tasks to assist classroom teachers in the instructional process. The positive value of cross-age tutoring is now widely recognized. In this setting volunteers can tutor students in small groups or individually.

The goals of NYS and secondary education are neither inimical nor mutually exclusive. Local school systems can become involved with NYS through its local administering agency and, in conjunction, create and operate efficient and effective youth-serving programs.

Academic Credit. The issue of academic credit for service experience is intertwined with the issues of educational linkages, particularly linkages to higher education.

In addition to the numerous ongoing educational dimensions of a service program, such as learning marketable skills and developing a work record based on sound work habits, a National Youth Service program must provide opportunity for formal academic credit and advancement.

Obviously, it would be inappropriate for the federal government to mandate a required amount of educational credit for NYS. However, three arrangements for academic credit should be part of any NYS program: a graduate equivalency diploma (GED), opportunity vouchers, and service learning. (The concerns about academic credit for out-of-school experiences are discussed in Chapter 2.)

1. Graduate Equivalency Diploma: Any youth entering NYS lacking a high school diploma should have the opportunity to obtain a GED. The tutors in such a program of assistance would include secondary school teachers and adult education teachers, as well as people from the NYS program. It is conceivable that, in the latter instance, a tutor who by day might be under the supervision of a non-GED person on a conservation gang, at night would be teaching the supervisor.

2. Opportunity Vouchers: The Commission recommends that serious consideration be given to incorporating an educational entitlement voucher – a type of GI bill for community service – into any plan for NYS. Under the terms of the opportunity voucher, those youth who serve X amount of time in NYS would be entitled to X amount of money from the federal government toward further education if they so desire. The logic of the Commission in proposing opportunity vouchers comes at a time when our population is decreasing and the cost of college is rising sharply, causing colleges to compete actively for students. Some form of educational entitlement for community service would appear to be infinitely sensible for bolstering our institutions of higher learning and, ultimately, our national economy through increased federal income tax payments. Additionally, this would provide colleges with a new source of mature students. Contrary to the fears expressed by higher education officials prior to the enactment of the GI Bill of Rights, students attending college following a period of military service proved to be mature, responsible, and academically superior students.

Opportunity vouchers should be based on the following formula: One year of educational entitlement will be granted for each year of NYS, up to a maximum of four years. Not everyone will utilize the opportunity vouchers in the same way. There is no time limit on the vouchers. Each individual will decide if, when, and how to utilize the vouchers. Regardless, the opportunity voucher will pay the published cost of the educational experience one chooses, ranging from medical school to study of the culinary arts, from barber school to airplane mechanic training.

3. Service Learning: An educational officer would play an integral role in every NYS camp or location. The officer would establish appropriate educational linkages for service participants. In addition to arranging for formal course credit, officers would also arrange flexible academic experiences encompassing learning clusters or packages. Such learning clusters or packages would be offered on a continuing basis rather than as formal courses.

For instance, arrangements could be made to bring a professional botanist or forester into a camp for a two-week academic session. Arrangements might also be made to bring service participants to a college campus for a summer institute. In such a setting, principles of forestry could be taught to participants. Such arrangements would add an entirely new dimension to an NYS program. It would give the program not only a measure of academic respectability but also an added important measure of social respectability.

Vast potential exists for higher education institutions in an NYS program. Such institutions can validate the experiences gained in service programs through accrediting and certification procedures. Particularly fruitful relationships can be established with community colleges and junior colleges because they are already oriented toward meeting the needs of their communities.

By administering projects, providing needed components of NYS, or even serving as prime sponsors of NYS projects, higher education can add validity to and enhance the NYS venture.

Wages to Participants. Sooner or later in most discussions of National Youth Service, a question of intent arises. Is NYS intended to serve the needs of the participants or the needs of the community and nation? This unidimensional question continually produces the simplistic answer, "Any way you look at it, one will be the by-product of the other." Perhaps the issue is not clear-cut.

Several arguments can be made on the issue of wages to be paid to NYS participants. One proposal is to pay subminimum wage rates for NYS work. This argument is based for the most part on the largely mythical adage that payment of a minimum wage runs counter to the grain of national service and voluntarism. The facts speak differently. Even in the existing volunteer programs that purport to pay participants on a subminimum scale, it was found necessary that the federal government intervene in one way or another. For example, an

ACTION survey of VISTA volunteers revealed that nearly half of them were being subsidized with government food stamps, thereby bringing them up to minimum wage levels.[21]

It must be recognized that the payment of a minimum wage to participants incurs the risk of building a self-defeating mechanism into any program for NYS. A small percentage of youth would be content to remain indefinitely in NYS programs, content to struggle on at the minimum wage, secure in the fact of perpetual employment on the public purse. To prevent such cases, the Commission suggests that no participant be eligible for more than four years of full-time participation in NYS.

Some will argue for the payment of prevailing wage rates to NYS participants on the grounds of equal pay for equal work. Proposals of this nature will kill the prospects of NYS. Even in the unlikely event that the proposal made its way through the Congress, demands would be made for the removal of the program out of the public sector into a privately developed program.

There are several compelling arguments for paying a minimum wage to NYS participants. The payment of a differential subsistence wage would mean only limited participation by minority youth in a service program. Payment of the minimum wage rate on the other hand would serve to dignify the program sufficiently in the eyes of minority youth and most likely encourage wider participation. It would also reduce the chances of the program being perceived by the middle class as mere tokenism or simply a handout to the poor.

In balance then, the Commission recommends the payment of the minimum wage rate and no more to NYS participants.

Labor Union Linkages. Whenever the issue of the kind and amount of remuneration is raised, the necessity for developing strong linkages with labor unions is recognized. If NYS is to be a reality, linkages with labor are a necessity. Without such arrangements, chances are slight that a proposal for NYS could make its way through Congress.

Labor support for NYS is possible if the proposal is based on the following assumptions and premises:

> Under no conditions do NYS workers replace paid workers.
> Wages paid to NYS workers will be at the minimum wage levels and be integrated fully into the nation's existing wage system, including withholding taxes. To avoid a situation where certain desirable jobs go to special groups, all NYS workers will be paid the same.[22]

Additionally, support from labor unions can be gained if the following are solicited:

> Involvement of union officials in the initial planning aspects of a program for NYS
>
> A union role in the training procedures of both supervisory personnel and participants in NYS

Finally, chances for union support for NYS can be enhanced considerably if the proposal is tied to a plan that could also provide employment for union members. Such mutual involvement is feasible. For example, if the Congress mandated that the Corps of Engineers conduct a massive cleanup of all of the nation's coastal harbors, rivers, and lakes, both union workers and NYS participants could play a role in the project.

Without question, then, if a program for NYS is to become a reality, the necessity for developing strong linkages with labor unions cannot be overemphasized.

Voluntary Versus Compulsory Service. To propose compulsion as a means to any end except the defense of life or liberty is to run the risk of rejection. In our pluralistic, open, free-wheeling, do-your-own-thing society, the expression "compulsory action" nearly always takes on pejorative meanings, conjuring up negative and antagonistic connotations in people's minds. For some, it runs counter to American democratic ideals. It is a complex issue; it is an emotional issue; it is a philosophical rallying point; and, for some, it is an obsession.

To assess the attitude of the public toward compulsion one has to look no further than compulsory education laws. These laws, which used to be rigidly enforced by truant officers, are still on the books of every state in the union. Yet, because of the public's attitude toward compulsion, they have gone the way of benign neglect. Principals, who are designated as the agents to enforce compulsory attendance, have enough problems without getting involved in the unpleasantness of compulsion; and, with the amount of crime in the country, it would be difficult to get a case of truancy on the dockets of the courts anyway.

Operating on the premise that the freedom of youth is the same as the freedom of adults, Commission members gave this issue more concentrated attention than any other. Despite the many complicating ramifications, the Commission was not deterred from confronting the topic head-on, nor did it attempt to avoid the issue of voluntarism. Entire sessions were devoted to the topic. Invariably, it reared its thorny, multifaceted head at nearly every meeting.

An appreciation developed among Commission members for the prophetic quality of Charles Bartlett's observation that National Youth Service is a program with a future, but an idea that "is so big and controversial that no politician knows how to get hold of it."[23]

Hours of lengthy testimony on the virtues of both compulsory and voluntary approaches were heard. Often testimony was accompanied by lengthy and deliberate debate. From this a scenario began to emerge, albeit very dimly. It resembled the medley: "I'm not saying that I don't like the idea of compulsory service for youth; rather, I am only pointing out that somebody else does not like the concept. But I like the concept myself."

Finally, the alchemy of two years of discussion on the topic began to yield results. It remained for a Commission member to place the vexing issue in perspective. Summoning nearly a half century of data that he had amassed on the topic of National Youth Service, Dr. George Gallup brought both insight and direction to his fellow commissioners. Speaking with clarity and from a position of personal conviction, armed with reams of statistical data to bolster his comments, he perceived the dilemma confronting the Commission in the following manner:

> When we first polled on National Youth Service, members of Congress said the church people would all oppose this. But when we went out and polled the church people we found they were just as much for the idea as everyone else. Congressmen are scared to death of National Youth Service. . . . Somehow, somewhere they have a feeling that parents will get mad at them and vote against them when they come up for election. But the public has been consistently in favor of this for almost forty-four years.[24]

Citing statistical results from polls dating back to 1935, Dr. Gallup revealed that the Civilian Conservation Corps is the most popular program ever sponsored by the federal government. It is the program that has received the highest degree of support from the American people over a fifty-year period. On the basis of the numerous Gallup polls on the topic, a CCC-type program invariably receives an approval rating from over 80 percent of Americans, never dipping below a level of 70 percent approval.

More revealing were the reactions solicited by Dr. Gallup from young people, aged eighteen to twenty-four, who would be most affected by a National Youth Service program. When asked their opinions about a compulsory year of national service of either a military or nonmilitary nature, opinion was nearly evenly divided – 50 percent in opposition and 47 percent favoring the proposition. Most revealing, however, was the finding that 40 percent of women favored some form of required National Youth Service for both sexes.

Fortified with this data, the Commission was determined to strike a delicate balance with its recommendations, not wishing to depreciate voluntarism by mandating compulsory service for all youth but equally concerned that every youth be guaranteed the opportunity to participate in the National Youth Service experience.

Accordingly, the Commission makes the following recommendations.

- The Commission recommends that the Congress enact legislation *requiring* all American citizens, both male and female, at the age of eighteen to *register* in their local community for the opportunity to participate in a National Youth Service program.
- The Commission recommends that local youth transitional planning councils (see Chapter 4) be designated as the mechanism through which compulsory registration shall be accomplished. In the event that there is no council operating on the local level, registration shall be carried out through the local Selective Service office.
- The Commission recommends that at the time of registration for National Youth Service, youth be given appropriate counseling on the full range of options available to them under NYS. These are service, work experience, occupational training, and educational opportunities.
- The Commission recommends that all employers – individuals, agencies, institutions, and businesses – in both the public and private sectors encourage youth to register and participate in the National Youth Service experience. The Commission especially solicits the support of the private sector to generate support for National Youth Service by advocating one year of service experience as a condition of employment.

As noted, the local youth transitional planning councils are the first choice of the Commission to handle the registration, with the local Selective Service office as the alternate. A dissenting opinion stated that using the Selective Service office could confuse National Youth Service with the draft in the mind of the public. The intent of National Youth Service to provide an opportunity if a young person chooses it could be misinterpreted. Yet the Commission as a whole considered the Selective Service office to be the logical choice to handle registration efficiently if there were no local council.

The Commission is aware that the constitutionality of the compulsory components of the proposed model for National Youth Service will most likely be challenged in the courts. The Commission welcomes action of this nature. The time has come for the Supreme Court of the United States to speak in definitive terms on an issue of such fundamental importance.

Military Conscription. The issue of voluntarism also raises implications for the national system of selective service. A decade ago, this was a major issue in any discussion of National Youth Service. Since the abolishment of universal military conscription, the issue has been defused.

One might speculate that the implementation of a program of NYS might have some unintended undesirable ramification on the All-Volunteer Armed Services. It is estimated that 40 percent of youth would choose military service as their choice of national service under a compulsory plan.[25] This would more than satisfy the current manpower demands of the armed services.

Implementation of National Youth Service

The name, National Youth Service, seems to connote a ponderous, centralized, heavily bureaucratized agency. It need not be. In fact, this conception is inimical to the effective functioning of a service program. Even though a program of such massive dimensions must be legislated by the Congress and funded in whole or part with federal monies, it need not be a heavily centralized program.

The numerous existing state and local programs, agencies, institutions, voluntary groups, and youth advocacy groups must be given careful consideration in implementing any program for NYS. Otherwise, NYS will encounter enormous opposition and ultimately will be subverted on the local level. Extreme care should be given to tapping into existing programs and resources on local levels. Void of widespread grassroots support, creativity ebbs in the development of creative programs. Local needs go unmet or are not addressed.

The great risk in legislating an NYS program is that it might be perceived as *the* single most important agency for youth. There could be a resultant slackening of interest and funding for the host of other agencies, as outlined in the previous chapter, that serve youth in the transition process in many important ways.

It must be recognized that successful implementation of an NYS program requires a carefully planned period of transition. It takes time to develop worthwhile jobs and work sites; it takes time to recruit supervisors; it takes time to develop policies that are tested pragmatically. All these factors are crucial to successful program development. If each of these concerns is not carefully addressed, large numbers of youth will be dumped out in communities that are ill-prepared to absorb them. Youth will be cast into menial and meaningless "make-work" projects that have little, if any, positive value for them.

Most of all, it will take time and a fair amount of imaginative tinkering to establish an appropriate prime-sponsor mechanism to administer NYS programs on the local level.

At the present time it would seem likely that if funds are appropriated by the Congress for NYS, they would be administered locally by existing CETA (Comprehensive Employment and Training Act of 1975) prime-sponsor mechanisms. The strength of the CETA prime-sponsor approach is that it utilizes a strong existing power base – the local mayor's office. It would be extremely difficult, if not impossible, to run effective NYS programs on the local level without the support of the mayors. An added benefit from this approach would be that it would not require additional bureaucracy.

There is, however, a major drawback to the CETA prime-sponsor approach. Most of the sponsors are presently totally unprepared and ill-equipped to plan, administer, and monitor the Commission's suggested projects. In many instances, if departments knew that they would be *guaranteed* large sums of money, there would be little incentive to change or improve on existing delivery systems. In other instances, departments would be simply unable to "tool up" fast enough to create effective and fiscally efficient NYS programs. In either instance, large amounts of tax monies would be squandered.

Another possibility would be to utilize ACTION as the administering agency on the federal level. This approach would offer two major advantages. First, ACTION has gained considerable operating experience in service-related programs through the Peace Corps, VISTA, and its two prototype programs for National Youth Service in Washington (PLS) and Syracuse (YCP). And second, ACTION enjoys a high image around the nation from professionals who work on a daily basis in service-related programs.

The Commission recommends that youth transitional planning councils (Chapter 4) play an active role on the local level in assisting and advising prime sponsors of NYS programs. In this role, youth transitional planning councils would operate under federal guidelines

but would enjoy considerable flexibility in order to respond more effectively to local needs.

Under this plan, local CETA organizations would funnel money to
youth transitional planning councils to oversee the NYS programs.
Neither the CETA agencies nor the youth transitional planning councils would run the programs on a day-to-day basis. In essence, CETA
agencies would subcontract their responsibilities for NYS programs to
the councils while still maintaining some control. The councils in turn
would act in an advisory and supervisory capacity to the actual sponsors of NYS programs.

Finally, there remains an additional means to facilitate and enhance
the implementation of NYS programs on the local level. When the
Comprehensive Employment and Training Act was passed in 1975,
Congress inserted a provision that has been often overlooked or simply ignored.[26] The Congress inserted a provision into the act allowing
CETA prime sponsors to deliver their resources to communities
through voluntary and nonprofit associations.

As pointed out in Chapter 2, voluntary and nonprofit associations
are an extremely important link in the transitional process of youth to
adulthood. Agencies such as the Boys' Clubs, 4-H, and the like are in
place and operating a variety of youth programs on the local level.
Community colleges and junior colleges are natural conduits for older
youth who would be attracted to NYS. In short, for many reasons both
voluntary associations and community and junior colleges are logical
sponsors for NYS programs. They command respect from the community at large; they enjoy the confidence of large numbers of youth;
they possess the proper temperament and degree of commitment for
NYS; they possess ample experience in a wide variety of youth-related
programs; and finally, they are staffed by extremely competent and
experienced personnel. NYS can benefit from the vast potential of
these organizations. They can and must play an important role in
NYS.

The Commission strongly recommends that the Congress, acting
under the provisions of existing CETA legislation, expand the provisions for voluntary and nonprofit agencies and institutions to participate as secondary sponsors of NYS programs.

The intent of the Commission is clear. Programs should be administered as much as possible at a grassroots level. Control of programs by a powerful centralized bureaucracy would be inimical to the
best interests of NYS. Under the coordination of the youth transitional
planning council, a variety of local agencies could be encouraged to
develop plans to implement various components of NYS. This should

lead to the development of a host of diversified, imaginative programs truly responsive to local needs of youth.

If NYS is to be perceived by youth as a genuine opportunity to render service to the community, then youth must not be cast in a passive role. To do so is to ignore a valuable source of creative input. Youth representatives should be involved in the developmental phase of program planning and be board members of youth transitional planning councils.

An Article of Faith

Social policy is the child of crisis. Such policy is not devised to anticipate crisis; it is developed in response to it. According to this viewpoint, the New Deal initiatives were inspired by fear and desperation and sustained by dire necessity. The only proven catalyst for social change is crisis and imminent catastrophe.[27]

A reflection of this crisis mentality is the tendency in the Congress to pass massive remedial measures "under the gun," then to sit back and say, "Well, that takes care of that problem."[28]

The point to be made is that there are several inherent limitations to short-term approaches to National Youth Service.

If NYS is perceived as the *single* most important institution for youth, there is great risk of slackening the emphasis on a host of other institutions and programs that serve youth in important ways. Creative programs for youth tend to ebb. Policies are designed and programs are implemented only to overcome immediate problems or crises. When the crisis disappears, the program becomes ineffective and is ended.

What is most alarming about this short-term approach is that all signs for the future point to greater changes in the nation occurring over shorter periods of time. We are a nation in flux. What works today is obsolete tomorrow. Thus, if we continue to embrace short-term approaches to youth problems and continue to procrastinate over the adoption of NYS, the implications are bleak – a treadmill of crash programs, poorly conceived, hurriedly assembled, and inefficiently managed.

As an alternative to this approach the Commission recommends that National Youth Service be established not as a short-term emergency program, but rather as a long-term continuing program. Such a program should stand as an enduring beacon of the nation's commitment to youth.

A commitment to National Youth Service will require an element of faith. Since we know more what to expect from NYS today than we did from the CCC and NYA forty years ago, the degree of faith won't have to be as great as that held by Eleanor and Franklin Roosevelt. But it must be comparable in character, for it will require faith in young people, faith in the government, and faith in the future.[29]

Notes

1. Diane Hedin and Byron Schneider, "Action Learning in Minneapolis: A Case Study," in Ralph W. Tyler, ed., *From Youth to Constructive Adult Life: The Role of the Public School* (McCutchan Publishing Corporation, Berkeley, Calif., 1978), p. 152.

2. Dan Conrad and Diane Hedin, "Citizenship Education through Participation," *Education for Responsible Citizenship*, report of the National Task Force on Citizenship Education (McGraw-Hill Book Company, New York, N.Y., 1977), p. 133.

3. *Service-Learning: A Background Paper, Bibliography, and Resource Guide*, ACTION Pamphlet 3530.1, Domestic Operations, New Program Development, April 1974, pp. 1-2.

4. Donald J. Eberly, "A Model for Universal Youth Service," prepared for the Universal Youth Service Conference sponsored by The Eleanor Roosevelt Institute, Hyde Park, N.Y., April 9-10, 1976, p. 7.

5. Donald J. Eberly, "Public Service Employment for Young People: A Review of Programs and Ideas in the USA," prepared for the Carnegie Corporation, September 1976, p. 2.

6. Franklin D. Roosevelt, Jr., and Joseph P. Lash, "The Roosevelts and National Youth Service," prepared for the Universal Youth Service Conference sponsored by The Eleanor Roosevelt Institute, Hyde Park, N.Y., April 9-10, 1976, p. 1.

7. Eberly, "Public Service Employment for Young People: A Review of Programs and Ideas in the USA," p. 3.

8. Roosevelt and Lash, "The Roosevelts," p. 2.

9. Donald J. Eberly, "Universal Youth Service Milestones, 1945-1975," prepared for the Universal Youth Service Conference sponsored by The Eleanor Roosevelt Institute, Hyde Park, N.Y., April 9-10, 1976, p. 1.

10. Ibid., p. 2.

11. Ibid., p. 3.

12. Remarks by Governor Aker, director, Youth Programs, Department of the Interior, at a meeting of the National Commission on Youth in Washington, D.C., April 28, 1978.

13. Eberly, "Universal Youth Milestones, 1945-75," p. 20.

14. "Washington State Creates Youth Service Corps," *National Service Newsletter* no. 33, Washington, D.C., September 1977, p. 2.

15. Harry J. Hogan, "National Service Now," prepared for the Universal

Youth Service Conference sponsored by The Eleanor Roosevelt Institute, Hyde Park, N.Y., April 9-10, 1976, p. 11.

16. Remarks by Robert Taggart, director, Office of Youth Programs, Department of Labor, at a meeting of the National Commission on Youth in Washington, D.C., March 2, 1978.

17. "Major Youth Employment Program Enacted," *National Service Newsletter* no. 33, Washington, D.C., February 1978, p. 1.

18. "Secretariat Invites Comments on New Youth Programs," *National Service Newsletter* no. 34, Washington, D.C., February 1978, p. 1.

19. Taggart, remarks.

20. B. Frank Brown, "A New National Policy Toward Youth," the Institute for Development of Educational Activities (/I/D/E/A/), Melbourne, Fla., unpublished paper.

21. Remarks by Donald J. Eberly, senior policy analyst for ACTION at a meeting of the National Commission on Youth in Miami, Fla., February 8, 1977.

22. Hogan, "National Service Now," p. 29.

23. Charles Bartlett, *Chicago Sun-Times*, April 7, 1967.

24. Remarks by Dr. George Gallup at a meeting of the National Commission on Youth in Washington, D.C., April 27, 1978.

25. The Gallup Poll, Princeton, N.J., January 20, 1977.

26. Hogan, "National Service Now," p. 33.

27. Willard Wirtz, "Universal Youth Service Conference: Summary Address," prepared for the Universal Youth Service Conference sponsored by The Eleanor Roosevelt Institute, Hyde Park, N.Y., April 9-10, 1976, p. 15.

28. Remarks by the Honorable Anthony J. Moffett, M.C., at a meeting of the National Commission on Youth in Miami, Fla., February 8, 1977.

29. Eberly, "A Model for Universal Youth Service," p. 28.

4

YOUTH TRANSITIONAL PLANNING COUNCILS: SMOOTHING THE TRANSITION

Recommendation 8: Establishing Youth Transitional Planning Councils on the Local Level. *Youth transitional planning councils should be developed in every community to smooth, shorten, and enhance the transition of youth to adulthood. Communities that are unable to sustain councils for lack of numbers or resources should establish regional councils.*

Recommendation 9: Membership and Status of Youth Transitional Planning Councils. *The mayor or chief executive of the community should appoint a cross-section of interested citizens to the youth transitional planning council. The council should be granted legal status and stand autonomous from local school boards.*

As our nation enters its third century, one is struck by the number of incongruities in our society. Human footprints on the moon are signal testimony of our capacity to overcome formidable obstacles. It would seem reasonable to assume that a nation that possesses the capacity to take "one giant leap for mankind" on the moon ought to possess similar capacity and desire to enable its youth to take "one small step" to adulthood in their own backyards.

The problem is not the lack of knowledge. Rather, it is the delivery systems we fashion to solve these problems. How does one transmit this knowledge and those ideas that we believe will work down to the community level? How do we get the data into the schools and factories, into the hands of teachers and employers, and into operation for the youth themselves?

The school, or any other institution for that matter, cannot function as the exclusive delivery system. The system must be based on a collaborative process, embracing a number of usually disparate entities—the schools, private industry, the public sector, a wide range of voluntary agencies and institutions, and youth themselves.

The greatest need, however, is to facilitate the development of such delivery systems on the local level.[1] To this end, the National Commission on Youth recommends the development of youth transitional planning councils. The council concept is the linchpin in the Commission's design for a new environment for the transition of youth to adulthood. These councils should be established in every community.

The term youth transitional planning council[2] admittedly lacks panache. It is not flashy. Neither is it arcane. It forms no acronym. Instead, it is distinguished only by its plain and straightforward qualities. It conveys precisely what the Commission envisages as its function: to serve as a delivery system to smooth and shorten the transition of youth to adulthood.

By definition, the council has a number of distinctive characteristics: it is an advisory board of legal standing; it is not concerned with schooling, but, rather, it gives public sanction and support to reconstructing the total educational system; and it is independent of the school board. Councils are composed of groups of citizens representing the community at large, organized for the purpose of smoothing and shortening the transition to adulthood. Councils achieve this goal by assessing the needs of youth in the community and identifying available resources in the community to meet these needs. In essence, the councils function as matchmakers or youth brokers, matching appropriate community resources to satisfy the needs of youth.

If communities are small or lack sufficient resources to provide all of the opportunities that should be available to youth, then councils should be established on a regional basis. Such councils would work to provide opportunities for youth on a regional basis that communities cannot provide within their borders.

Characteristics of Youth Transitional Planning Councils

Youth transitional planning councils have tripartite functions: first, they are mechanisms to expedite the transition of youth to adulthood; second, they have a mission to make the transition go more smoothly; and, finally, they provide a method that utilizes collaborative processes, bringing together community resources to meet the needs of youth.[3]

Some Underlying Assumptions

Virtually every community is rich in resources—personnel, institutions, agencies, and industries—to assist youth in the transition to adulthood. With such abundant resources, one might ask why isn't more happening? The answer is simple. Most communities lack the requisite collaborative processes to make more productive use of their resources. This collaboration can't happen by federal mandate or by similar legislative fiat. It must come from the grassroots level. Much interest has already been expressed on an informal basis, embracing a variety of groups involved in a wide spectrum of programs and activities. But this interest must be channeled into a common effort. People and programs that have operated separately must be brought together in a collaborative effort to serve youth more effectively.

Interconnections of this nature cannot be made simply by establishing yet another youth program. The key, rather, is better integration of existing local programs. This is the role youth transitional planning councils must play in the socialization of youth. Capitalizing on local community initiatives, the councils can infuse the transitional process with the knowledge and experience that rests in the broader community.[4]

To summarize, the concept of youth transitional planning councils is based on the following assumptions:

The local community is primarily responsible for tending to the transition of youth. Transitional problems of youth cannot be successfully resolved without community involvement.

The need for widespread community involvement is crucial. Rather than placing the onus for transition of youth on a handful of professionals, such as teachers, guidance personnel, and employment counselors, the responsibility must be shared by the community at large.

Presently, many programs function as separate entities. Instead, what is needed is increased cooperation among, and better integration of, existing personnel and programs.

Community Involvement in Councils

It is safe to assume that in most communities across the nation, there are action-oriented, highly motivated citizens willing to serve as advocates for youth. Organized into youth transitional planning councils, these citizens could act as third-party interventionists and exercise considerable influence on the dynamics of community groups through the following functions:

Identify and define problems in manageable proportions
Serve as conveners of interested parties
Provide a forum for community opinion

Function as proxies for disparate community groups
Provide linkage between important sources of power and influence in the community
Legitimize goals and directions for institutions and agencies involved actively in the transitional process
Provide general leadership for youth interests[5]

People serving on the councils, either as individuals or as surrogates for institutions and agencies, are those citizens who are in the best position to contribute input to, and exercise significant influence on, the transitional process in the community setting. Obviously, the particular mix of individuals serving on the councils will vary in each community. Some obvious candidates are

Youth representatives
Parents
Employers
Labor union officials
Teachers
School guidance counselors
Employment counselors
Public-spirited citizens[6]

Incentives are needed to attract the best-qualified people as council members. One benefit would be the vast brokerage potential councils possess. They could transform what are often adversarial relationships between institutions, agencies, and individuals into collaborative efforts to serve youth. Additionally, councils must have the power to effect change, including control over funds.

Councils as Youth Advocates

Youth transitional planning councils must function as advocates for youth. Many of the institutions that youth encounter in the transitional process to adulthood are subjected to the pressures of a variety of constituents. The result is that commitments to youth are slowly compromised and ultimately eroded. Youth development is consigned to a low priority. For example, companies that in former times may have hired a large percentage of local youth for their labor needs may now be severely constricted in their hiring practices as a result of featherbedding practices of labor groups. In fact, most industrial enterprises lack any long-term commitment or allegiance to youth. Another example involves the sovereign worlds of employment and schooling. The prospects for increased cooperation appear dim, except as some kind of third-party advocacy-type force is brought to bear on the separate entities. An advocacy function of this nature entails serving as a broker to youth.

As advocates, the councils will be going wherever the action is, working to identify potential resources and linking them to the needs of youth. Thus, the advocate role encompasses not only delivering services to youth but also becoming a liason between such established institutions as schools, businesses, governing bodies, and labor unions.[7]

The advocacy function of youth transitional planning councils is a free wheeling one. It is also far-reaching in scope. Consequently, it demands that councils function as boards of total educational planning.

Councils as Boards of Total Educational Planning

The councils must view the transitional process in the widest possible sense. This macroscopic view entails the following functions: an analysis of the total resources of the community; a determination of what needs to be done to make these resources more responsive to the needs of youth; and, finally, the recommendation of policy to facilitate this end. In short, the councils' scope of responsibility is the *total* educational environment.

The policies and practices developed by councils will necessarily be evolving, individualized, varied, and specific. The changing needs of youth as well as community priorities and constraints demand flexibility. Although it is not possible to delineate these practices in infinite detail, a general outline is possible.

• Councils can improve community understanding of the problems that youth encounter in making the transition to adulthood. This might seem trite, but people in general, along with parents, don't always grasp the problems that youth face in trying to make the transition.

• To facilitate community understanding, councils can hold community hearings where parents, concerned citizens, community leaders, and representatives of youth service organizations are brought together to talk about the kind of support youth need from the local community to make successful transitions to adulthood. Young people themselves can also be brought in to discuss their frustrations, what they perceive as their problems, and what they would like to do about them. Hearings of this type would raise the levels of public consciousness, making the community more closely attuned to the problems of youth.

- To develop more accurate data on youth needs, councils could initiate youth needs assessment surveys. In most communities, the employment service cannot give an accurate account of the unemployment rate for youth of varying age groups. And if one requests employment data on subgroups within the community or on specific neighborhoods, absolutely no data on these configurations exist.[8]

- Councils can inventory and make information available on the range of youth service programs that already exist in the community. This aggregated data can then be developed into youth service directories or directories of current community programs and activities.

- A better match between the needs of youth and the available resources to meet these needs can be achieved by establishing and monitoring clearinghouse functions. Thus, the councils would survey and, of course, develop additional experiential opportunities and oversee the matching of these opportunities in the community with young people's needs.

- Councils can develop and monitor opportunities for youth to obtain exposure to adult environments, such as worker service experience, plant tours, attendance at union meetings, or observing workers in specific jobs. In addition, arrangements can be made for representatives from various trades and professions to come into the classroom to talk to youth about work.

- Councils can also identify and attempt to overcome barriers that currently exist between education and work or that keep youth from gaining alternate educational experience in community-based settings. Such barriers include poor understanding or rigid interpretation of labor laws; concern about employer liability insurance; concern about funding formulas based on average daily membership; concern about class scheduling and related administrative procedures in secondary schools; and, finally, concern about the potential of youth displacing adult workers from jobs or having an otherwise adverse impact on the wage structure of the community. Youth transitional planning councils would serve to facilitate discussion of these issues, improve the accuracy and the level of understanding of these issues, and introduce an element of flexibility in the community at large about the value of such practices.

- Finally, councils can serve as forums where people representing different constituencies in the community can come together and get help in defining what their interest is in helping young people. Subcommittees could be formed in the councils to handle such tasks as developing a policy on community-based education.

Relationship of the Councils to Secondary Schools

It must be underscored that the broad mandate of the youth transitional planning councils does not diminish in any manner the standing of secondary schools. To the contrary, secondary schools are strengthened, not diminished, by the councils' mandate.

This point was emphasized repeatedly throughout the Commission's deliberations by Robert McGee and William Saunders, representatives of the public schools serving on the National Commission on Youth. Secondary schools should help prepare youth for employment and assist in the placement of youth in jobs, but "they must reassert and reserve their major energies for teaching the traditional academic pursuits."[9] Left to pursue traditional academic goals, secondary schools would actually become less vulnerable to much of the criticism currently leveled at them, particularly in regard to the quality of vocational programs.

School boards will retain their traditional responsibilities for administering secondary schools. The business of school boards will continue to be the schooling of youth. Youth transitional planning councils, by contrast, focus on the *total* educational environment, of which schooling is but one part. Thus, school boards and councils complement each other. They share a common aim, however, in that both assist youth in the transition to adulthood.

The youth transitional planning council has the same relationship to the secondary school as it has to a business corporation, to a service agency, to a hospital, or to a governing body. All are valuable community resources utilized by the council to smooth, shorten, and enrich the transition of youth to adulthood.

The Need for Legal Autonomy

It must be recognized that the past history of the council movement is not impressive. This is hardly surprising, given the conditions under which most councils operate on local levels. Most councils are doomed from their inception because they lack the requisite legal standing.

There are several compelling reasons to grant legal standing as autonomous bodies to youth transitional planning councils. One is philosophical, the other political.

Philosophically, if the councils are placed under the jurisdiction of school boards, many community institutions, agencies, and groups that currently function as important resources for youth – private schools, parochial schools, sectarian agencies, and the like – would never feel accepted as full partners in any cooperative enterprise.

Politically, it must be recognized that school boards and the educational apparatus are among the most powerful bureaucracies operating on the local level of government. To place the youth transitional planning council under the jurisdiction of the school board would render it impotent in all but name. The school apparatus would quickly dominate it and eventually transform it into yet another administrative division of the schooling process.

For these reasons, the Commission recommends that youth transitional planning councils be granted legal standing and be made independent of school boards. As free-standing, autonomous bodies, councils would have legal sanction to operate in a total community environment but would not be dependent for their continued status on any of the institutions and agencies that operate in that environment. Such autonomous status would allow councils to negotiate relationships between various community sectors and interests. Councils could operate simultaneously as catalysts to prod segments of the community into action and as brokers or matchmakers bringing people and institutions together to better meet the needs of youth.

Ultimately, the philosophical and political issues boil down to two questions: Who shall have the responsibility for the transition of youth to adulthood? The answer is simple – the entire community. And who would appoint representatives of the community to the councils? All factors considered, the mayor or chief executive officer of the community is the logical choice.

Operating Characteristics of Youth
Transitional Planning Councils

The easiest part of establishing councils on the local level will be the enlistment of volunteers. Individuals, along with representatives of institutions, agencies, and businesses, will give their time to help young people. The councils will provide a forum for their interests. Employers, for example, have at least a general interest in youth. Very often, however, it is difficult for them to relate that interest to their corporate goals and objectives. The same thing is true with labor unions.

Membership in youth transitional planning councils will enable people at the local level to sort out their interests in youth. No mandates will come from Washington about why employers should be interested or why labor unions should be involved in the councils. Rather, these mandates are the expressions of citizens on the local level who find their own reasons for involvement.

A number of related questions come to mind at this point. With so many advisory councils presently operating on the local level, why the need for another? Why would this group be any more effective than other advisory councils? What kinds of things would youth transitional planning councils do that existing councils or agencies are not presently doing?

Youth transitional planning councils would be unique in a number of ways from existing advisory councils operating on the local level. This unique standing stems from the following operating characteristics:

• The council's working agenda would reflect consistently the community's own sense of priority. It would be hoped that various local interests would be impelled to play an active role in the council, thereby reflecting accurately the full range of community attitudes.

• Councils would be concerned with the development and implementation of policy regarding a particular *problem*, not any particular *program*. The problem, of course, is the transition of youth to adulthood. Thus, the councils pose no threat to existing programs nor are the councils committed to a specific approach or allied to a particular program. Indeed, their mission is just the opposite, trying to enlist the aid of as many approaches and programs as possible to smooth the transitional process.

• Councils would move beyond a concern with day-to-day administration of any specific programs, with one exception. As noted in the previous chapter, if National Youth Service becomes a reality, councils might serve as agencies to register youth in the program. By and large, the councils would focus on broader issues. For example, what are the implications, if any, for the transition of youth if schools operate on a year-round basis? Would a year-round school system tend to help or hinder opportunities for community-based education? If industries move into town or leave town, how will this affect job opportunities for youth?

• Councils will not have a direct affiliation or association with or be funded by a CETA or YEDPA institution or constituency. Instead of competing for these funds, the councils will serve as conduits of funds to youth agencies. One example of this is the relationship outlined in Chapter 3 between the youth transitional planning council, the CETA prime-sponsor mechanism, and a National Youth Service program.

• Councils may serve as direct advisers to youth and on occasion may advocate a particular approach to dealing with youth. Examples of these in Chapter 2 include vocational education, career education, and the like.

The collective impact of the councils, however, is intended to be greater than the sum of the parts outlined above. The intent is not to compete with existing programs and agencies but rather to infuse understanding and awareness into the community of the problems that youth encounter in the transition to adulthood.

Council Secretariat

At the local level, a small professional staff or secretariat is necessary to assist the council in the performance of the functions listed above. The secretariat would help the council perform these functions through various means: gathering data from the community, assessing youth needs in the community, inventorying community resources, and cataloging local programs related to the transition of youth to adulthood. These activities have a twofold purpose: to inform both council members and the community at large about youth needs and to identify the resources that are available in the community to meet these youth needs.

The secretariat gives a certain degree of continuity to the council's functions. It contributes an ongoing dimension to the council. Additionally, the secretariat functions as a mechanism to lever support for programs and agencies already in place.

It must be recognized there is an inherent danger in the secretariat proposal. Once the secretariat function is fully implemented, councils can attract so much support that there is a danger that they will evolve into another superagency, mired deep in bureaucracy. At this point, councils would lose much of their effectiveness, succumbing to the self-serving syndrome endemic to all bureaucracies.

The intent is to keep the salaried staff small, funding it at a modest level. From $30,000 to $50,000 should be sufficient to maintain the secretariat on an annual basis.[10]

Youth Delivery Systems

Historians write of the "Law of Unintended Consequences," which twists the simple chronology of history into scenarios that are not at all intended. No one can doubt that it was a serious error for American citizens to disengage so completely from traditional civic duties. The quality of life has deteriorated in thousands of communities as a result of this apathy. At least some of the circumstances that bedevil youth today are an unintended consequence of our lack of community involvement and commitment.

We have reached a point in our period of introspection where we are beginning to realize the enormous price we have paid for our lack of commitment. Perhaps we are on the very threshold of a turning point in our national history, characterized by a renewal of civic commitment and a rededication to the young.

Concern for the welfare of the young and pride in their accomplishments used to be a cohesive force for many communities. If we have indeed finally emerged from our long stasis, these forces can once again become the rallying points for a new community spirit. Youth transitional planning councils can be the means to achieve this catharsis.

Capitalizing on this new-found awareness, youth transitional·planning councils can become a familiar part of the community landscape across America. Prototypes of the organization envisioned by the Commission are already in place. Operating under the aegis of the National Manpower Institute, they exist in such places of high youth unemployment as Buffalo, New York, and Oakland, California; similarly, they are operational in Lexington, Kentucky, and Charleston, South Carolina, where there are low rates of unemployment among youth. They can also be found in metropolitan areas like Philadelphia, Pennsylvania, and in rural locations, such as Bethel, Maine, and Martin County, North Carolina. In short, a mechanism is being developed to deliver valuable services for youth in a wide variety of places under vastly different circumstances.

But beyond all of these things, overriding them all, will be the benefits that will flow into every community if the councils can become the means to put local people in communication with each other around a common set of problems—the problems confronting the young of their communities.

Focusing on the total educational environment that has been so eroded in recent times, councils can coordinate all the important sectors of the community that are potential learning centers for youth—industry, government, service institutions, and youth organizations. Then they can encourage and oversee these organizations, institutions, and groups as all sectors work toward smoothing, shortening, and enhancing the period of transition to adulthood.

They can, in short, serve as delivery systems to enable youth to take "one giant leap" to constructive adult lives.

Notes

1. Willard Wirtz et al., *The Boundless Resource: A Prospectus for an Education-Work Policy* (New Republic Book Company, Washington, D.C., 1975), p. 20.

2. The National Commission on Youth acknowledges, with gratitude, the work of the National Manpower Institute, Washington, D.C., for the general outlines of this concept.

3. Dennis Gallagher, "The Work-Education Consortium: A Progress Report," *The Work-Education Exchange*, vol. 2, no. 2, National Manpower Institute, Washington, D.C., March-April 1978, p. 1.

4. Wirtz, *The Boundless Resource*, p. 65.

5. Luvern L. Cunningham, "Citizenship Participation: Lessons for Citizenship Education," *Education for Responsible Citizenship*, report of the National Task Force on Citizenship Education (McGraw-Hill Book Company, New York, N.Y., 1977), p. 158.

6. Wirtz, *The Boundless Resource*, p. 66.

7. Ibid., p. 65.

8. Remarks by Dennis Gallagher at a meeting of the National Commission on Youth in Chicago, Ill., December 16, 1977.

9. Remarks by Robert McGee at a meeting of the National Commission on Youth in Washington, D.C., April 28, 1978.

10. Remarks by Dennis Gallagher at a meeting of the National Commission on Youth in Chicago, Ill., December 16, 1977.

PART 2

NEEDS OF YOUTH

5

YOUTH AND UNEMPLOYMENT

Recommendation 10: Youth Unemployment Policies. *The focus of government policies to reduce youth unemployment should be twofold. Short-term policy initiatives should concentrate on the* cylical *and* frictional *aspects of youth unemployment in order to ameliorate undue suffering and hardship among unemployed youth, while long-term policies should focus on the* structural *aspects of youth unemployment in order to reduce persistently high rates of unemployment among the young.*

Recommendation 11: Payment of a Differentiated Wage to Youth in Training. *Payment of less than minimum wage should be made to youth who are gaining job training and experience in apprenticeships, internships, and job-training programs.*

Payment of a subminimum wage to youth in training can create incentives for private employers to develop and expand carefully supervised programs.

Performance-based training grants, tax write-offs, and wage tax deferments can provide additional incentives to stimulate training programs in the private sector.

Recommendation 12: Improvement of Youth Employment Services. *The Bureau of Labor Statistics should take steps to develop more reliable statistical data on the scope of youth unemployment.*

Concomitantly, state governments should develop local and regional data that reflect more accurately the rate of youth unemployment in local settings and among different concentrations of youth.

Along with these efforts, the U.S. Employment Service should establish a youth section to better serve the employment needs of young people.

Recommendation 13: Revision of Child Labor Laws. *Federal and state governments should launch a coordinated effort under the U.S. Department of Labor to revise the entire body of child labor law. Such revision is needed to better safeguard the health of young people on the job and to open up additional avenues of employment through the deletion of anti-quated statutes and regulations.*

"I like to have money," exclaims Terry Pickens. "It's nice to have money instead of being flat broke all of the time. Most of my friends are flat broke," he observes.[1] A young newsboy, aged fourteen, realizes for the first time in his life what most adult Americans have known for a long time. Work gives people a sense of dignity, a self-respect that adds a sense of purpose to life.

The notion that people have a desire for – and many believe, a right to – dignified, meaningful work is echoed over and over in Studs Terkel's best seller, *Working*, which details the innermost frustrations of more than 300 working people across the nation.

But significant numbers of Americans are denied the opportunity to become masters of their own lives and to feel that their work and they themselves are important. Instead, for some, chronic unemployment is becoming a way of life. By far the most affected are youth. Young Americans, aged sixteen to twenty-four, constitute one-quarter of the national work force but account for one-half of the total unemployment. A disproportionate fraction of these are members of minority groups.

The job needs of youth vary greatly. Most youth, aged sixteen to eighteen, are still in school and seek part-time or seasonal work. Their needs are not generally crucial. By contrast, a crisis exists for youth between the ages of eighteen and twenty-one. Most have completed high school and some have even acquired college degrees. Many are ready to embark on careers or to assume family responsibilities, but they are unable to find jobs commensurate with their abilities and training.

For another segment of youth, those who have failed in or have been failed by the educational system, it is a disaster. Most need extended assistance of a comprehensive nature.

Finally, if one is a member of a minority group and falls into the previous category, it is a catastrophe. Significant numbers of youth in this category have stopped looking for jobs. Some have already abandoned hope for productive adult lives and are resigned to the prospect of living by their wits. Left to their own devices and failing in their attempts to establish linkages with the world of work, they will instead establish linkages with detention centers and prisons.

No statistics, however, can adequately describe the long-range damage to the political, social, and moral fabric of America when a substantial portion of young citizens have no productive role in life.

Many economists maintain that even with a substantial upturn in the economy, joblessness for the young will persist in high numbers. Glorious youth, which should be a time for putting the finishing touches on one's values and character, is engendering hopelessness, despair, and cynicism for many of the young who cannot obtain jobs. Youth unemployment is not a problem. It is, rather, a disgrace and a growing national scandal.

Considering both the magnitude of the present numbers of unemployed youth and the future implications of this trend, relatively little attention has been given to the issue. Some officials continue to insist that youth unemployment is not really a national problem. Some see it as transitory. It is not.

One cannot expect that all young people who are disillusioned by the American economic system will, as adults, be turned on to the virtues of the American political system. Youth who are denied the opportunity to share the economic fruits of the nation might not participate in the political process as adults. If youth unemployment continues at its present record-breaking levels, America may reap a bitter harvest in future years in the form of millions of adults lacking in all sense of social and political responsibility.

No one can state with certainty the consequences of prolonged economic dependence on future generations of adults. The National Commission on Youth believes that America runs an enormous risk by continuing a policy whereby substantial numbers of unemployed and underemployed youth are maintained solely from public and familial largess.

Some of the consequences of such policies are already evident. Rehabilitative institutions, both criminal and mental, are literally bursting from record numbers of clients. A disproportionate number of the incarcerated are under the age of twenty-five. Delinquency and crime rates among the young have reached very high levels. Most tragic of all is the suicide rate for Americans between the ages of sixteen and twenty-four, a rate that has doubled in the past ten years to the present rate of 17 percent—17,000 per 100,000 youth. Both of these disturbing trends will be analyzed in depth in subsequent chapters in this section of the report of the National Commission on Youth.

How did we arrive at the present condition? Many of these problems are the problems of success.[2] America has become the first nation in history that could continue to increase its gross national product over a sustained period of time without relying substantially on the manpower of its youth under the age of twenty-one.

We have become a society increasingly dominated by economic rationality and a growth-and-consumption ethic. Chronic unemployment problems and education are tied to jobs in a way that leads ineluctably to overcredentialing, with low-goal consensus and little willingness to look at the realities of our long-term youth problems. If present trends continue, the future holds no panacea for youth.

Importance of Work in the Transitional Process

Sparse attention has been paid to the value of work in the transition of youth to adulthood. This is surprising, since work may well be the single most important factor in the transitional process. Work has the following redeeming qualities:

> Teaches discipline and personal responsibility
> Provides a source of financial independence
> Expends time and energy in a purposeful manner
> Creates a sense of social identification and status
> Constitutes a source of meaningful life experiences

When these qualities are added to two needs that are an integral part of human growth and development – the need for self-respect and for the respect of others and the need to express one's self creatively – work indeed becomes the means for successful transition to adulthood. Work has the capacity to fulfill both of these important human needs.

Because work is the activity around which most adults organize their lives in order to establish a productive and rewarding routine, it must loom large in any effort to smooth and enhance the transition of youth to adulthood. In order to underline the importance of the work ethic in American society, one only has to view the lives of men without work – and the absence of a sense of purpose that people have when they do not have work as a way of life. We are, in short, a work-centered society.

The Nature of the Problem

The problem of youth unemployment can be subdivided into cyclical, frictional, and structural factors.

Cyclical factors, by definition, are those that directly or indirectly affect the supply and demand for youth labor. The supply of youth labor is affected by such variables as the total number of young people between the ages of sixteen and twenty-four, their moves in and out of the labor market, and the level of competency they bring to their jobs. Demand is influenced by the general condition of the economy along with the need for specific types of labor skills.

Among some of the more important cyclical factors that contribute to youth unemployment are the following:

> Abnormal growth in the teenage population between 1955 and 1974
> Increase in the number of youth seeking full-time and part-time work
> End of universal military conscription
> Decrease in the manpower needs of the military
> Recession of 1973 to 1975[3]

In addition to these cyclical factors, a nominal amount of frictional unemployment has always existed among youth. Such frictional factors are an inevitable part of the transition of youth to adulthood. Frictional factors are defined as those variables that impel youth to seek or to leave jobs as they make their initial entry into the labor market. A period of testing, during which youth get their feet wet in the labor pool, is a necessary trade-off between the need for individual freedom and upward mobility and high unemployment rates for youth. This is the price that must be paid to ensure initial access to the labor market and subsequent freedom of choice and job mobility for youth.

There is, however, considerable evidence that the current high rate of youth unemployment is neither a frictional necessity nor a cyclical aberration. It is instead a structural phenomenon. Structural factors are persistent, long-term, and only minimally influenced by market conditions. Structural factors are recession-proof. Long after the final effects of the recession have faded, high levels of youth unemployment will remain.

As pointed out in Chapter 1, opportunities for youth to do productive work have been decreasing steadily as the school has been isolated from the world of work. Lack of emphasis on learning related to the world of work is one, but probably not the most serious, structural factor. This is indicated by the substantial numbers of well-qualified youth who cannot find work simply because there are no jobs available.

A number of other variables contribute to the dimensions of the problem. Among the more important structural factors are the following:

Technology
Entry of large numbers of women into the labor market
Minimum wage laws and levels
Restrictive practices that have been bargained into labor contracts
Current lack of incentives for employers to incur large fixed training costs associated with job training programs for youth
Regulations imposed by government and unions
Deferred retirements by older workers
Longer period of unemployment for adult workers
Decline in economic growth which slows down creation of new jobs

These structural factors drive home a very important point. Youth unemployment is always going to be significantly higher than the level of adult unemployment. All projections for the future point to a youth employment rate under "normal" economic conditions of 8 to 10 percent.[4] For all practical purposes in the foreseeable future, this figure will be indicative of full employment for youth.

It is apparent to the National Commission on Youth that we need to explore the possibility that youth unemployment is only one aspect of a more fundamental problem. We need to consider the possibility that we are dealing not with a temporary crisis associated with a temporary recession but, rather, with a society moving toward a significantly altered system. In short, the variety of youth problems associated with the transition of youth to work might be generated to a large degree by the structural problems of a society that is itself in transition. The utility of taking this broad perspective may lead us to an infinitely more realistic understanding of the evolutionary change in society itself. Any particular measures undertaken to solve the problems of youth unemployment must be chosen to fit in with the shifting pattern of the whole.[5]

To date, most federal programs have been short-term efforts, focusing on the amelioration of youth unemployment through the creation of artificial jobs. By and large these programs fail to address the more basic structural causes of the problem.

In this light, the National Commission on Youth recommends that the focus of government policies to ameliorate the problem of youth unemployment be twofold: short-term policies should focus on the *cyclical* and *frictional* aspects of youth unemployment in order to eliminate undue suffering and hardship among unemployed youth; and long-term policies should focus on the *structural* aspects of youth unemployment in order to reverse or to adapt more effectively to long-standing societal trends.

The Statistical Dimensions of the Problem

The impact of the 1973 recession on youth employment was catastrophic. What was initially seen as a brief period of cyclical discomfort for youth has now become a prolonged nightmare. Life is no longer a bowl of cherries for substantial numbers of American youth. Rather, it is decidedly "the pits."

Youth unemployment increased from 14.3 percent during the final quarter of 1973 to 20.5 percent during the second quarter of 1975.

The number of teenagers and young adults who were unemployed during 1976 averaged almost 3.5 million, nearly half the total numbers of jobless Americans. Unemployed youth between the ages of sixteen and twenty-four account for 42.6 percent of all unemployment. In 1977, a monthly average of 3.3 million young people under the age of twenty-five were looking for work. This represents approximately one-half of the nation's official unemployment rate as determined by the Bureau of Labor Statistics (BLS).

If the recession has turned out to be a depression for youth in general, it is catastrophe for minority youth in particular. The economic recovery has barely affected minority youth, leaving them with unemployment rates in 1978 well over twice the national average. In many major urban centers across the nation, minority youth unemployment runs as high as 50 percent.

These statistics represent only part of a very bleak situation. Hundreds of thousands of youth, their lives broken and disrupted, have despaired of finding productive work and have simply stopped looking. These casualties are no longer counted in the official statistics. The National Manpower Institute estimates that there are currently 600,000 youth who have dropped out of the labor market. The truth is nobody really knows the precise dimensions of youth unemployment. Statistical figures on youth unemployment are tenuous at best.

The vagaries of the initial entry of youth into the job market tend to obfuscate Bureau of Labor Statistics figures. To cite several examples, some youth seek work only in the summer and then return to the educational world. Growing numbers of youth now earn and learn simultaneously. Some of those listed as unemployed may also be full-time students. The official BLS figures are especially ambiguous for minority groups, particularly for black and Spanish-speaking groups. (The bureau stopped compiling statistics on the basis of race in 1971.)

There is a certain grim irony to the present situation. Although the Bureau of Labor Statistics is acknowledged throughout the world as a model of accuracy and efficiency, it is unable to provide reliable statistical data on the nature and extent of youth unemployment in the local ghetto. The present measurement system is designed to illuminate the adult unemployment picture. The problem is not lack of data. The Bureau of Labor Statistics, the Office of Education, the Census Bureau, and the Employment and Training Administration have assembled reams of statistics on youth unemployment. The problem is that the data need sharper focusing on the transitional period to adulthood as it relates to youth in local labor markets.[6] The local community is where most youth make their initial entry into the labor market.

As consensus grows for combining the now distinct realms of learning and earning, traditional labor statistics have even less meaning. The current data base needs considerable supplementation along the following lines:[7]

• More data are needed on the amount and kinds of work experience youth are gaining. This includes not only paid work experience but also the entire voluntary and service sector. In short, the whole experiential component needs careful measurement.

• Schooling, experience, and training are the major vehicles of transition from a status of youthful dependence to a status of adult independence. Currently, the training component is virtually ignored by quantifiers. School enrollment statistics are too narrowly focused. They should be broadened to include private schools, apprenticeships, formal training programs provided by private employers, and a wide variety of CETA-related programs.

• Greater differentiation should be given to age levels in statistical data. From a purely statistical point of view it is reasonable to lump together aggregate data on sixteen- to twenty-one-year-olds. It does nothing, however, to illuminate the transitional process. One year can mean a profound difference in the attitudes and habits of the young during the critical transitional period of life. In order to yield greater insight into the transitional years, statistical data should be broken down into one- to two-year aggregates. These aggregates must be defined further by data relating to degree of dependency, educational status, marital situation, and number of incomes in a family.

• An increasing percentage of youth pass through various institutions – military, penal, health – during the transitional years. Yet, statistical data on the institutional population are virtually ignored, although this information is vital to determine the general condition of any society. It is imperative that generalizations on the status of youth be drawn from information about the total youth population.

• There is an acute need for longitudinal studies on youth.[8] The Census Bureau's annual October Survey of High School Graduates should be strengthened to obtain additional data on the nature of the wage and work experiences of students who graduate from high school but do not attend college. The 1966 National Longitudinal Survey of Men and the National Longitudinal Survey of the High School Class of 1972, both targeting on ages fourteen to twenty-four, should be continued. Particular emphasis should be placed on the work-study experiences of noncollege-bound students.

It would seem reasonable that a nation whose puerile interests include such data as the length of travel records by foot, dog sled, and submarine would be similarly interested in the length of the unemployment queues formed by their sons and daughters. A sad reflection on our sense of national values is that the *Guinness Book of Records* is a best seller while the monthly Bureau of Labor Statistics releases on youth unemployment are largely ignored. We know much more about the price of hog futures and pork bellies than we do about the characteristics of youth unemployment.

The National Commission on Youth recommends that the Bureau of Labor Statistics take immediate measures to develop more reliable statistical data on the scope of youth employment. Concomitantly, individual states should develop youth employment data with local and regional capacities in order to (1) report more accurate rates of youth unemployment in local settings and among different concentrations of youth, and (2) make both long-term and short-term forecasts of job availability and outlook, particularly at the entry level of employment.

The Psychological Costs of Youth Unemployment

Unemployed youth, like school dropouts, make interesting statistics. But numbers alone cannot convey what it means to a youth not to be able to find a job. It is impossible to measure the impact of involuntary idleness on the human spirit. How does one measure such nebulous concepts as self-esteem, self-development, and hopes for the future?

Some commentators argue that youth unemployment is not a serious problem because most youths are not principal breadwinners. The National Commission on Youth rejects such observations. The problem is immediate and serious, and it will not solve itself automatically as youth grow into adults. The future implications are most distressing. Failure to confront the problem now will mean that at some future point it will be necessary to rehabilitate significant numbers of middle-age adults who drifted for a decade or more without ever acquiring significant work experience.

Unemployment constitutes a serious waste of human resources. At any age it can be an indelible blight on human existence. When it affects youth, it carries additional consequences. The first missed opportunity, the deflating impact of being laid off or discharged from a job, the debilitating effect of standing for hours in an unemployment line to claim benefits, the destruction to the human spirit incurred by aimless drifting with neither purpose nor hope for the future, the feigned lethargy or cavalier attitude that masks growing inner doubt and eroding self-confidence – all these can scar a young person for life.

The remarks of Secretary of Labor Ray Marshall put the costs of youth unemployment in proper perspective:

> The work habits and attitudes formed early in life last a lifetime. Workers who are unable to develop marketable skills in their late teens and early twenties often have difficulty finding employment for the rest of their lives. Most young workers enter the labor market insecure about their abilities and worried about whether they will be able to make a meaningful contribution to their society. A protracted period of joblessness can erode their self-confidence and sense of individual worth. This experience can give rise to psychological problems, marital difficulties, and even suicide.
>
> The despair and hopelessness produced by youth unemployment can damage the social fabric. The credibility of any society depends in part on its ability to provide meaningful work for those willing to work. For those entering the job market, an inability to find work tends to weaken the credibility of that society.[9]

Defining the Barriers to Youth Employment

Youth unemployment is not merely a straightforward economic issue. In addition to economic considerations, the political, social, and psychological aspects of the problem are both complex and varied. Among these are the following:

> Attitudes of employers, labor unions, and youth themselves toward employment
> Behaviors of key institutions that do not necessarily reflect the existing forces in the marketplace

Isolation of major socializing institutions from each other that impedes the transition from school to work

Various laws and institutional rules that create barriers to youth employment

Massive influx of illegal aliens that siphons jobs from both youth and adults alike

Various disincentive factors for employers including minimum wages, liability insurance, and fringe benefits[10]

All of these factors, along with a host of others, are interrelated. All can provide a disincentive for employers to hire youth between the ages of sixteen and twenty-one.

Employer Perceptions

Corporate hiring policies toward youth are neither positive nor negative. They are nonexistent. A 1973 study conducted by the National Manpower Institute characterized corporate attitudes toward young workers as follows:

Local conditions are the major variables in hiring youth.

Most youth unemployment is temporary, caused by students seeking part-time work and by new entrants into the job force.

Higher youth unemployment is a permanent feature of the the capitalistic system.

More youth will be hired if they become more competitive with adult workers in terms of productivity and costs.

Compared with adult workers, youth are less disciplined in basic work habits, change jobs more often, are more militant, and have higher rates of absenteeism.

Increased numbers of youth coming into the labor force fail to have basic literacy, mathematical, and communication skills.

Youth are more likely to advocate for union representation and then to push for higher initial wage increases.

Youth are not as well organized or as vocal as minorities, women, and veterans.

The disadvantages of youth are self-correcting with time.[11]

Some of the viewpoints expressed above are obviously misconceptions about youth or are not substantiated by existing data. Despite these misconceptions, employers are generally supportive of efforts to hire youth. Historically, the private sector has contributed considerable monies, resources, and expertise to resolving the problem of youth employment.

Youth Attitudes and Aspirations

The work ethic is alive and well among American youth. Contrary to popular sentiment, most young people want a job and do not have an inherent dislike for work. This is borne out in a recent Gallup poll.[12] When youth were asked if they had a job lined up for the summer months, nine out of every ten teenagers indicated that they either had a job or would like to have one. Of the teens polled, 47 percent were already working at jobs or were firmly committed to a job for the summer months.

Labor-force participation rates for eighteen- and nineteen-year-old males increased from 69 percent in 1965 to 73 percent a decade later.[13] More impressive was the gain noted among females in a similar age category, rising from 49 percent in 1965 to 58 percent in 1975.

The facts speak for themselves. Youth are not lazy. All evidence points to the contrary. The National Commission on Youth believes that it is high time that this shibboleth be put to rest.

The Commission notes, however, that there appears to be a growing dichotomy between the career aspirations of youth and the types of jobs that are available to youth. James Coleman observes that while this trend is not limited to black youth, it tends to be more pronounced among minority youth in comparison to their white counterparts. The schools in low-income areas may be responsible for this.[14] By encouraging minority youth to stay in school longer, schools invariably raise the career aspirations of students.

Union Attitudes

Unions, like employers, have played a role in programs to alleviate youth unemployment. As noted in Chapter 2, unions have participated in a variety of training programs enabling youth to gain valuable work experience and providing jobs for unemployed youth. Among the more noteworthy examples are a number of Job Corps programs and the Job Opportunities program under private-sector sponsorship.

Despite this record, it would be correct to assume that unions do not regard youth employment as a top priority. The interests of older workers, who constitute the rank and file of union membership, consistently take priority over the needs of youth. It is fair to say that current union response to federal training and employment programs for youth has been mixed. Local unions, particularly, have restrictive policies toward apprenticeship and training programs, designed to protect the interests of their membership; by contrast, national unions tend to be more receptive to innovative training and job programs for youth.[15]

State and Federal Laws

Unlike the previously listed barriers to youth employment, legal barriers have a high degree of visibility. They can be classified into two categories: child labor regulations, which determine who may work; and minimum-wage regulations, which determine the financial conditions of employment.

Child Labor Laws

A plethora of state and federal regulations, often overlapping in nature, establishes the conditions under which youth may be employed. The major function of these laws is to protect youth from working conditions that jeopardize their health and safety.

As pointed out in Chapter 1, the genesis of these laws is most interesting. A major part of their inspiration stems from the desire to prevent the exploitation of youth by mandating compulsory school attendance. As a result, many of the present child labor laws are closely linked with compulsory school attendance regulations. Before youth under the age of sixteen can apply for work, it is necessary to secure work papers or permits from school authorities. These permits attest to such factors as age, physical fitness, and the level of educational attainment.

Although no one seriously challenges the necessity and the function of child labor laws, considerable disagreement exists over the degree to which they serve the overall interests of youth. Specifically, a case is made for more frequent reexamination of the occupations and conditions that are designated by law as being hazardous to youth.

Perhaps we have reached a point where many of these laws no longer serve the interests of youth but, rather, protect adults from the competition of youth for jobs. The ideology that inspired these laws is still very much alive, particularly in such groups as labor unions and a number of youth service organizations. Society in general and the world of work in particular have changed drastically in recent decades, but a good deal of the cumbersome ideology remains intact, embodied in antiquated, conflicting, and often confusing state and federal laws.

In order to systematize and update child labor laws to more effectively serve the needs and the interests of youth, the National Commission on Youth recommends that state and federal governments launch a coordinated effort under the direction of the Department of Labor to revise the entire body of child labor legislation. Such an effort should serve to safeguard the health of youth and, at the same time, to open additional avenues of employment through the deletion of antiquated statutes and regulations.

Minimum-Wage Laws

Bring up the subject of minimum-wage laws in a discussion and you are certain to hear spirited and prolonged debate. Employers cite it frequently as the chief deterrent to youth employment. Yet any suggestion to alter minimum-wage legislation sparks instant controversy. The labor unions would be among the last to yield on the issue, precisely because they initiated much of the existing wage legislation.

The National Commission on Youth did not escape controversy on the minimum-wage issue. Numerous sessions (Appendix A) were devoted to forceful and lucid presentations by acknowledged experts in the field of labor law and youth employment. Hours of spirited debate were devoted to thrashing out the many ramifications of minimum-wage laws. Several Commission members presented position papers on the subject. From all of this, a fragile colloquy took shape. From this colloquium, consensus emerged. Unanimity was not achieved among the Commissioners, nor was it to be expected.

At face value, the resolution of the minimum-wage issue appears simple: by imposing a minimum wage, the government prices substantial numbers of youth out of the labor market. The solution then is simple: abolish the minimum wage for youth, thereby opening more jobs for youth. Like most problems of a socioeconomic nature, however, once the thin veneer of simplicity is dispelled through sustained analysis and debate, a complex and multifaceted issue is found beneath. This issue proved to be no exception.

The effect of a minimum wage on employment patterns remains very much in contention, with empirical studies often contradicting one another. The parameters of the argument can be stated as follows: to the extent that minimum-wage laws force employers to pay higher wages for youth than the available work justifies, those laws reduce the demand for youth labor. Because minimum-wage laws do not apply to all jobs, some youth displaced from the covered sector may obtain employment in jobs not covered by the laws. But as long as some youth do not obtain new jobs, youth unemployment rates will rise and the total number of youth who are employed will remain steady or will decline.[16]

The impact of minimum-wage laws is especially detrimental to minority youth. In fact, there is the hint that a higher minimum wage attracts additional white youth into the labor market while discouraging nonwhite youth.[17]

A number of equally compelling arguments can be made in favor of paying minimum wages to youth.[18] If minimum wages for youth are reduced, adults who are heads of households are most directly affected. Cheap youth labor is simply substituted for more expensive adult labor. A 1975 study prepared for the U.S. Department of Labor by Dr. Alan Fisher of George Washington University estimates that additional employment of 800,000 teenagers will result in the unemployment of approximately 500,000 adults. In balance then, the payment of a differentiated wage to youth would seem to produce a mixed effect: it would undoubtedly reduce the youth unemployment rate, but it might increase the adult unemployment rate.

While recognizing that the payment of a subminimum wage to youth would undoubtedly raise youth employment rates, the Commission is painfully aware of the repercussions of any such action. The gains of youth would most likely be made at the expense of adult workers at the lower end of the prevailing wage scales. The impact would be particularly acute on women and minority workers.[19] A trade-off of this nature is too distasteful for the Commission to accept.

The minimum-wage issue must be evaluated in its total context rather than in terms of its effects on either youth or adults. Democracy is not a one-way street. Social and economic justice cannot exist in a vacuum. It must exist for both youth and adults alike. As citizens of equal standing, both groups are entitled to no more and to no less. Blaise Pascal, the French philosopher and mathematician, once noted, "a man does not show his greatness by being at one extremity, but rather by touching both at once."

The National Commission on Youth recognizes that the private sector has contributed considerable monies, resources, and expertise to resolving the problem of youth employment. The Commission also recognizes that the private sector cannot by itself be expected to continue these efforts indefinitely or to initiate major new efforts without substantial long-term financed commitment from the government in support of such initiatives. If the private sector is to enlarge some of the work training and experience ventures that are outlined in

Chapter 2, government incentives must be provided to make such programs economically feasible.

As a necessary first step in this direction, the National Commission on Youth recommends the payment of a differentiated wage to youth who are gaining work training and experience in apprenticeship and internship programs.

The National Commission on Youth also recommends that federal and state governments provide incentives to the private sector on a continuing basis in order to stimulate the development and enlargement of programs to give job training and experience to youth. Incentives can be provided through the expansion of such mechanisms as job training allowances, tax write-offs, and tax deferments.

Consideration of the minimum wage issue places one ultimately in a position of being caught between an acerbic critic and a passionate lover. One must question national values and priorities when forced to choose between the alternatives of paying subminimum wages to youth or displacing significant numbers of adult workers who labor at or slightly above the minimum wage level.

At prevailing minimum-wage rates, it costs slightly over $1,000 per year to employ a youth two hours per day on an annual basis. Forty million youth, aged sixteen to nineteen, could be hired at an annual cost of slightly more than $40 billion. This constitutes a substantial sum, for certain, but it is about equal to the amount that the country spends annually on tobacco and alcohol. Above this is the realization that alcoholism costs private industry close to $100 billion in lost revenues on an annual basis, while smoking costs the nation an additional $9 billion in related costs for forest fires, building fires, and increased insurance premiums. When one considers that the U.S. Department of Agriculture spent $65 million in price supports to the tobacco industry in 1977, one is hard-pressed to conjure up reasons that would justify deviating from the long-standing practice that wages are determined by the nature of the job and the quality of the work performed.

Smoothing the Transition to Jobs: Some Prescriptive Proposals

There is no panacea that will solve the unemployment crisis for youth. Jobs alone will not solve the problem. What is needed is a broad range of strategies that will meet the varying needs of different youth constituencies. A broad, flexible, and comprehensive approach must be adopted. Some youth need only jobs; others need to acquire or to upgrade basic skills; still others need personal and occupational counseling.

A comprehensive approach must focus on the transitional process in particular, on the antecedent educational structure, on the consequent employment structure, and, finally, on the social ills of the nation in general.

The prescription of the National Commission on Youth, embodying both short-term and long-term components, calls for the following twelve strategies.

1. There must be a substantial increase in the number of jobs available for youth. This need is particularly acute for inner-city minorities. Population projections indicate that the volume of young people under the age of twenty-four will not begin to decrease until 1985.

Despite some of their failings, it is imperative that job programs stemming from President Lyndon Johnson's Great Society programs, like the NYC and Job Corps, be continued. The Neighborhood Youth Corps (NYC), a much maligned institution, has been an important source of income for those youth who have no other means of support. The NYC has supplied many jobs to youth, sometimes simple and menial work but frequently very worthwhile work. The Job Corps, in particular, despite the frequent public criticism leveled at it, has been the single most important institution in absorbing those youth who are in the greatest need.

2. In September 1978, Congress passed legislation extending CETA job and training programs for four more years with greater emphasis on youth and tighter controls against fraud. The bill, which cost $10.9 billion for FY 1979, will create more job and training programs for youth and will increase the programs designed to place unemployed youth in jobs in the private sector.

The National Commission on Youth believes that a necessary first step for the Congress should be to correct the flagrant abuses and fraudulent practices that have characterized the program and to give private industry the significant role it must play in any massive training program.

3. As previously noted, the 95th Congress took steps to address structural unemployment through the enactment of the Youth Employment and Demonstration Projects Act in August 1977. The Carter administration has requested a slight increase ($300 million) in YEDPA funding for FY 1979. This should be appropriated.

4. In the waning days of the 95th Congress, final action was taken on the Full Employment and Balanced Growth Act. Known as the

Humphrey-Hawkins Act, the measure is designed to provide a framework for developing and implementing a coherent, coordinated national employment policy. Specifically, the act proposes to reduce unemployment to 4 percent by 1983 and, at the same time, to reduce inflation to 3 percent.

Some Commission members note with approval the act's mandate that the order of priority of job expansion programs should be through the private sector, using appropriate tax and monetary policies. Others see the act as an ill-conceived move toward more federal intervention in private sector activity.

At this point, the implications of this legislation for youth employment are still unclear. Some members of the Commission think it will create more problems by hampering the private sector in coping with unemployment of all kinds. In any case, it remains to be determined if the Carter administration's commitment to the Humphrey-Hawkins Act is more substantive than symbolic.

5. Private employers and labor unions must step up their efforts to assist youth in need of jobs, particularly those in the major urban centers. Unions in particular are finding that when Job Corps centers are run properly in collaborative efforts with private employers, they are superb screening places to recruit new minority members.

The Phoenix Job Corps center, which opened in 1969, is an example of a particularly successful program. Operated by Teledyne Inc., the center is a model for future program development. In addition to training young people in new types of job skills, heavy emphasis is placed on developing such personal habits as punctuality and neatness that will help trainees hold jobs.

6. The National Alliance of Businessmen must increase its efforts to involve the private sector in job programs for youth. The present program has never completely recovered from the effects of the 1973-1975 recession. It can be a valuable conduit for funds to the private sector for costs associated with youth training and employment programs.

7. A particularly difficult problem is the design of appropriate systems to give wage subsidies. Can this be done most effectively through employers, through unions, or through agencies?

One approach might be to give private employers subsidies in the form of tax credits. Tax deductions to business are granted for captial investment and improvements. On the same basis, similar incentives can be given to the private sector for introducing apprenticeship and internship programs for youth, flexible time programs, job training programs, and specially targeted minority training programs.

Wage subsidies to private industry as solutions for youth employment may be helpful in the short run but not in the long run. Two defects in subsidies are evident. While the subsidy lasts unemployment declines, but if it is temporary, the business normally is unable to absorb the extra cost and unemployment for the young people returns. Whether or not the subsidy is made permanent, the added cost becomes an added tax burden on business that finds its way necessarily into the cost of goods produced and the cost of living. And the cost is greater than if it were incurred directly by business, by virtue of the added costs of government handling of the funds.

Tax incentives come closer to being a constructive way to aid the private sector in solving unemployment. Every act of government that reduces the cost of government also eases the tax burden and may thus encourage business growth.

The National Commission on Youth recommends the use of federal taxation policies for creative social purposes. This approach could provide an entirely new motivational dimension to resolving the problem of youth unemployment, something quite different from the standard motivational tactics used by the federal government at the present time. Private industry would have something that could be depreciated over a period of time for tax purposes and, at the same time, provide an invaluable service to youth.

8. National Youth Service and community service programs should be implemented on a long-term and continuing basis. Youth would benefit immediately from the jobs in which they would be placed. The nation and the communities would benefit from the labor performed by youth.

9. Action-learning programs must be developed along the lines of those efforts outlined in Chapter 2. Expansion of these programs will lead to better integration of education and work.

10. Any comprehensive plan must include upgraded informational, counseling, and placement services. No one knows the types of jobs that are available for youth in local labor markets, let alone what types of jobs will be available on the local level in the next five to ten years. Local training opportunities for youth also need to be identified.

11. When proper informational services are in place, the next step is placement in an appropriate job. But placement services for youth making their initial entry into the labor market are generally lacking. Schools do not consider student placement as their responsibility. The U.S. Employment Service does not relate well to youth. The efforts of the U.S. Employment Service to assist youth into the labor force have

deteriorated to the point where they are practically nonexistent. As a result, young people make their initial entry into the labor market on their own.

The National Commission on Youth recommends that the U.S. Employment Service increase its efforts to assist youth into the labor market. A first step should be the creation of a special youth section within the employment service.

12. The focus of school counseling programs must be broadened to include increased numbers of students who choose to begin working rather than to continue their education. Schools today have neither the resources to make career education a priority in the curriculum nor are counselors competent to advise youth on careers in general and the local employment situation in particular.

The Career Education Act recently enacted by the Congress is encouraging. Under a system of matching grants to states, the act is designed to stimulate career education by instructing more teachers and counselors in the career information they should be transmitting to students. The National Commission on Youth applauds these efforts to infuse career education into the school curriculum and urges continuation of these efforts.

Pulling It All Together

Most of all, there is a need for some kind of community-based mechanism to fit all the pieces together in order to smooth the transition from the classroom to the production line. Neither mandates nor money can accomplish this. It can be brought to fruition only by cooperative efforts on the community level among disparate organizations, agencies and institutions, and individuals that exercise control over some segment of youths' lives and opportunities. In short, an active partnership is needed on the community level among labor, education, industry, the voluntary sector, parents, and youth themselves.

This message came through loud and clear at a January 1978 White House conference on balanced growth and economic development. Calling youth employment a built-in form of "social dynamite," Reginald Jones, chairman of the board of the General Electric Company, stated: "We need new institutional arrangements, a new organizational framework at the local level, a new spirit of cooperation. Everybody's got to pull together—government, business, labor, education, community agencies, minority organizations. We've all become too ingrown, too concerned with our own particular interests and procedures."

The National Commission on Youth believes that we can begin pulling it all together now through the establishment of youth transitional planning councils. It is an organizational framework uniquely suited for this purpose.

Notes

1. Studs Terkel, *Working* (Pantheon Books, New York, N.Y., 1972), p. xli.

2. Excerpted from a presentation by Willis W. Harman to the National Commission on Youth at Cornell University, Ithaca, N.Y., on May 11, 1977.

3. *The Quiet Crisis: A Report on Unemployment Among Young Californians* (Open Road/Issues Research, Citizens Policy Center, Santa Barbara, Calif., 1977), pp. 31-32.

4. Remarks made by Dr. Sar Levitan, George Washington University, to the National Commission on Youth at a meeting in Miami, Fla., on February 8, 1977.

5. Harman, presentation.

6. Paul E. Barton, "Youth Transition to Work: The Problem and Federal Policy Setting," *From School to Work: Improving the Transition*, a collection of policy papers prepared for the National Commission for Manpower Policy (U.S. Government Printing Office, Washington, D.C., 1976), p. 13.

7. Ibid., pp. 14-15.

8. Richard Freeman, "Teenage Unemployment: Can Allocating Educational Resources Help?" *The Teenage Unemployment Problem: What Are the Options?*, report of Congressional Budget Office Conference, October 14, 1976 (U.S. Government Printing Office, Washington, D.C., 1976), p. 47.

9. Ray Marshall, opening statement, Organization for Economic Cooperation and Development, Paris, France, December 15, 1977, p. 3.

10. As quoted in David Goldberg et al., *Youth and Work*, Youth Development Program, University of Colorado, HEW Grant no. 79-HD-85003/8-05, August, 1975, pp. 21-22.

11. Patricia Marshall, "Corporate Attitudes Toward Young Workers," *Manpower*, Vol. 5 (August 1973), p. 28.

12. Gallup Youth Survey, Princeton, N.J., June 8, 1977.

13. Sar Levitan, "Coping With Teenage Unemployment," *The Teenage Unemployment Problem: What Are the Options?*, report of the Congressional Budget Office Conference, October 14, 1976 (U.S. Government Printing Office, Washington, D.C., 1976), p. 63.

14. James Coleman, *The Teenage Unemployment Problem: What Are The Options?* p. 49.

15. Goldberg et al., *Youth and Work*, p. 26.

16. Remarks of Dr. Jacob Mincer, professor of economics, Columbia University, and Dr. James Ragan, economist, Federal Reserve Bank of New York, at a meeting of the National Commission on Youth in Washington, D.C., September 16, 1977.

17. Ibid.

18. Remarks of Dr. William Buechner, staff economist, Joint Economic Committee, U.S. Congress, at a meeting of the National Commission on Youth in Ithaca, N.Y., May 11, 1977.

19. Edward Gramlich, "Impact of Minimum Wages on Other Wages, Employment, and Family Incomes," *Brookings Institution Papers on Economic Activity*, vol. 2 (Washington, D.C., 1976).

6

YOUTH CRIME
AND DELINQUENCY

Recommendation 14: Television Violence. *The viewing public should continue to pressure the television networks and their local affiliates to assume increased responsibility for decreasing the levels of crime and violence on television to which youth are exposed.*

Recommendation 15: Reform of the Juvenile Justice System. *The present system of juvenile justice should be reconstituted along new lines. The key is to differentiate within the existing system.*

Courts should continue their efforts to separate serious offenders from less serious offenders. The use of nonincarcerative sanctions—fines, restitutions, community service—should be encouraged for less serious offenses.

Finally, if rehabilitation is the primary objective of the juvenile justice system, a wide array of remedial services must be provided to meet the needs of youthful offenders.

Recommendation 16: Prevention of Youth Crime and Delinquency. *Efforts to prevent youth crime and delinquency should focus on early levels of intervention and diversion. Preventive measures will have maximum impact when they are brought to bear on the environments in which youth operate—the home, the school, the neighborhood, and the community. Whenever feasible, youth offenders should render an appropriate form of service to the neighborhood or to the community as a form of restitution for criminal offenses.*

Recommendation 17: Elimination of Status Offender Classification. *The courts should cease the practice of classifying youth as status offenders. The jurisdiction of the juvenile court system should be limited to those acts that if committed by an adult, would constitute a criminal offense and to dependent and neglect statues, which allow the courts to intervene in order to protect the health and welfare of young people.*

Adults have always felt that children get away with murder. But what was formerly a hackneyed expression is now all too literally true. Youth crimes are not pranks. They are felonies ranging from murder to rape and include larceny, violent assault, and armed robbery.

Youth between the ages of ten and seventeen account for only 16 percent of the national population, but persons under the age of eighteen constitute approximately 50 percent of the arrests for serious crimes. Between 1960 and 1974, youth arrests for all crimes jumped 138 percent. Most alarming, however, was a whopping increase of 254 percent during the same period in youth arrests for the most violent index crimes—murder, rape, robbery, and aggravated assault.

The Dimensions of the Problem

A sense of the magnitude of youth crime is gained by analysis of the proportion of different crime arrests attributed to particular age groups. The 1975 crime statistics are most revealing: Eighteen-year-olds were the most arrested (6.6 percent) group in the nation; the second highest group was seventeen-year-olds, then nineteen-year-olds, followed by sixteen-year-olds.[1]

It is said often that most kids are good, and only a few troublemakers spoil it for the rest of youth. This is true. Only 3 percent of the total youth population between the ages of ten and seventeen are officially judged delinquent by the courts.[2] While most youth at some point in their lives commit at least one delinquent act, they are not caught and go on to lead crime-free lives.

Even fewer youth become habitual offenders. This trend is confirmed by a longitudinal study of 10,000 Philadelphia youth who were born in 1946 and lived in the city between the ages of ten and eighteen. Those youth arrested four or more times constituted just 6 percent of the original group, but they accounted for 52 percent of all youth crime.[3]

A final persistent trend is that disproportionate numbers of low-income, inner-city youth are arrested for a wide variety of crimes. The incidence of arrest for recidivists in large cities is 2.5 times greater for youth from low socioeconomic backgrounds than for youth from high socioeconomic areas.[4]

These statistical trends are alarming and significant. The most vital statistics on youth crime, however, cannot be measured in quantitative form—the ruined lives, the dashed hopes, the loss of personal security, and the terrible waste of human resources resist numeration.

Causes of the Problem

Youth crime is like cancer. There is much that is not known about the causes, the remediation, and the prevention; but the effects of both are highly visible and equally devastating.

The theoretical underpinnings of the relationship between crime and delinquency and its causes also remain clouded. Various factors, including economic, social, and cultural variables, are equated with youth crime and delinquency. For example, street crime is considered a substitute for youth employment. Vandalism becomes a creative antidote to a drab school curriculum. Defiance of parental authority is viewed as a preface to more serious forms of defying the law.

Recent studies on the subject are illuminating but not definitive. For example, the prestigious Hudson Institute[5] concludes that such deterrents as the light sentences that are imposed are chiefly responsible for the huge bulge in youth crime. But respected sociologists like Paul Friday and Jerald Hage,[6] positing from a much broader perspective, emphasize the critical role of socializing processes and the criminative effects of peer-group associations. Criminality, they conclude, is the result of the breakdown of the traditional ways in which societal values are transmitted to young people.

Television, Crime, and Delinquency

The uncertainty among experts as to the causes of youth crime and delinquency is most certainly not shared by parents. While scores of studies by psychologists and sociologists have left unclear the relationship between television viewing and the rise of youth crime and delinquency, ask any group of parents what causes youth crime, and television is invariably cited as one of the chief culprits.

What gives parents this certainty that experts fail to achieve? A 1972 report by the surgeon general of the United States provided the credulity that eluded the experts. The report found a tentative causal relationship between television violence and aggressive behavior among young viewers. Citing no less than fifty studies to conclude that "what you see is what you get," the report quickly became the rationale of the movement for reform of the television industry.

Television has become the new article of faith for Americans. In times past, things were so "because I read it in the newspaper." Now reality is ascribed to by the quip, "I saw it on television." The National Commission on Youth believes that the impact of television on the lives of the young should not be minimized. Because of the breakdown of many of the traditional agents of socialization such as the home, religious institutions, and schools, television plays an increasingly prominent role in the formation of attitudes and beliefs of youth.

The fact that television has become the new article of faith for youth is hardly surprising. By the age of eighteen, many youth have logged over 15,000 hours in front of the television set compared to only 11,000 hours in school. Many youth are addicted to television, requiring a daily "fix" of at least several hours. By the age of fourteen, the average youth witnesses 11,000 murders on television. A steady diet of crime viewing, day after day, year in and year out, takes its toll. Many youth are convinced that manipulative and assaultive behavior is a standard method of problem solving.

The young are not the only group to be influenced by the formidable powers of television. Television viewing has become literally a lifelong curriculum, influencing learning and behavior from the womb to the tomb. It has become the first centralized cultural influence to dominate the initial and final years of life as well as the years between.[7] So varied are the powers of television, it can occupy young and old alike with equal facility.

Television is also a unique instrument of socialization. Unlike the medium of print, television makes no demands on basic literacy. Unlike the local cinema, television never closes. What's more, it is free. Not only is it free, but it even comes right into the living room in living color.

Television Violence

In his book, *The Two Worlds of Childhood*, Commission member Urie Bronfenbrenner notes that children are increasingly turning to television characters as behavior models. The National Commission on Youth views this with concern. While it may be discomforting to imagine the young identifying with television role models who inspire and glorify violence, admittedly the potential exists.

A recent article is both persuasive and disturbing. Grant Hendrick, himself an inmate at Michigan's maximum security prison, goes directly to the source and offers some startling conclusions. Hendrick conducted an informal survey of 208 of his fellow inmates, asking them what they felt about the correlation between the crime and violence they see on television and the crime and violence they practiced as a way of life. He outlines the connection: "A surprising nine out of ten told me they have actually learned new tricks and improved their criminal expertise by watching television programs. Four out of ten said that they attempted specific crimes that they saw on television crime dramas, although they also admitted that only about one-third of the attempts were successful."[8]

Various groups and individuals around the nation have studied the effects of television violence on young people. The American Broadcasting Company commissioned a massive study of 10,000 New York, New Jersey, and Connecticut youth, aged eight to thirteen, over a five-year period. The study asked participants to punch an electronic gadget before and after viewing television violence. Predictably, the participants hit harder after exposure to television violence. In addition, a nine-year study by George Gerbner and Larry Gross at the University of Pennsylvania concludes that "network policy seems to have responded in narrow terms, when at all, to very specific pressure, and only when the heat was on."[9] While the networks have displayed a tendency to change, they have not done so either drastically or uniformly. The study notes that the networks have curtailed the incidence of violence during "family hours" viewing, but this tends to be canceled out by a sharp rise in the incidence of violence during children's shows and in the late evening hours.

Much of the credit for recent pressure brought to bear on the networks belongs to two organizations – Action for Children's Television (ACT), a Boston-based group, and the Parent-Teacher Association (PTA). A recent two-year study of television violence by the PTA offered the following conclusions.

> Television violence contributes to aggressive behavior among youth.
> Some youth commit violent acts in direct imitation of violent acts they view on television.
> Violence is often portrayed on television as the best or the only solution to conflicts.
> The painful consequences of violent responses are underplayed.
> There is growing desensitization among youth to violence.
> The perception of youth of real-life problem-solving methods is distorted by certain television programs that fail to illustrate proportionally nonviolent methods such as discussion and compromise.
> Youth who view television violence on a regular basis are more fearful of real life.[10]

The controversy still rages over the precise impact of television violence on youth. The National Commission on Youth believes that a number of observations, based on existing evidence, are in order.

The Commission is unalterably opposed to government censorship or any abridgement of First Amendment rights. The Commission believes, however, that the license to broadcast bears with it concomitant responsibility to produce programming that meets community interests and concerns. It is the responsibility of the public to keep the television networks informed of these needs. The National Commission on Youth recommends that the public bring increased pressure to bear on both the networks and their local outlets to assume responsibility for decreasing the levels of crime and violence in television programming.

We are at a point in cultural history where the potential of television, for better or for worse, is in the balance. While other existing structures, such as the family and school, decline and lose influence in the socialization process, television increases in prominence and in importance. Conversely, as these structures are either rejuvenated or reconstituted, television will decline in its impact on the transition of youth to adulthood. It must be recognized that the potential of television as an educational tool for the betterment of youth is as great as the possibility of television becoming a detriment to the young.

The words of E. B. White point us in the direction in which the balance should tilt. "Television should arouse our dreams, satisfy our hunger for beauty, take us on journeys, enable us to participate in events, present great drama and music, explore the sea, the sky, and woods and hills. It should state and clarify the social dilemma and the political pickle. Once in a while it does, and you get a quick glimpse of its potential." This is the challenge before us. Above all else, if this potential is to be for the better, there is need for continuous public concern. No longer can the public react as a passive sponge, content to allow television to lead us where it may, secure in the belief that in the end things will turn out for the best.

School Crime

Much has been said and written about the problem of crime, violence, and vandalism in the public schools. Public consciousness of the problem was raised to a new height in 1975 by Senator Birch Bayh (D-Indiana), chairman of the U.S. Senate Subcommittee to Investigate Juvenile Delinquency. In a report entitled *Our Nation's Schools—A Report Card*, Senator Bayh noted that "the number of American students who died in the combat zones of our nation's schools between

1970 and 1973 exceeds the number of American soldiers killed in combat throughout the first three years of the Vietnam conflict." He went on to point out that between 1970 and 1973 school crime increased by the following dimensions:

> Vandalism now costs taxpayers about $600 million annually.
> Assaults on students increased 85.3 percent.
> Assaults on teachers increased 77.4 percent.
> Robberies in schools increased 36.7 percent.
> Rapes increased 40.1 percent.
> Confiscation of deadly weapons increased 54.4 percent.
> Murders increased 18.5 percent to 100 per year.

Reaction to the report by Senator Bayh was typically mixed: teachers assert that the problem is more serious than outlined by the statistics; school administrators, however, maintain that the problem is not as serious as indicated by the report. One thing is certain: the issue can no longer be evaded. We are at a point in public education where we are trading significant amounts of money for school security that were formerly spent for instructional purposes. Funds that formerly were spent to hire teachers to facilitate the process of instruction are now used to hire security guards so that instruction may take place. The facts speak for themselves. The Philadelphia Public Schools Security Force has become the second largest police force in the Commonwealth of Pennsylvania. In New York City, public school security expenditures jumped from $500,000 in 1970 to over $15 million in 1974. The best-kept secret in many school budgets is the amount of money that is spent for school security and to repair the damage of vandalism.

Because of the incidence of crime, violence, and vandalism in the public schools, Congress requested that the Department of Health, Education and Welfare, through its research arm, the National Institute of Education, conduct a major study of the problem.

The Safe School Study

How serious is the problem? It is most serious, according to the results of the study.[11] Acts of crime, violence, and vandalism increased steadily from 1960 to 1975 and appear to have leveled off at 1974-1975 figures.

Most disturbing is the finding that *secondary schools* have become the most dangerous place for youth to spend their time. Although youth spend only 25 percent of their waking hours in school, 40 per-

cent of the robberies and 36 percent of the assaults on urban youth occur during the school day. The problem is not confined to large-city
schools. Although urban schools reported the greatest proportion (15
percent) of serious crime, four out of five schools reporting serious
crime problems were in suburban and rural areas.

The National Commission on Youth concludes that security and
discipline continue to be serious problems in the public schools. Nor
can there be any argument that increasingly larger proportions of
school budgets are being expended to curtail vandalism and establish
a measure of order in secondary schools.

The Commission suspects that one of the major reasons that crime
and vandalism rates persist at alarmingly high levels is the attitude
among certain state legislatures and the courts that public education is
a fundamental right that cannot be forfeited or abridged. One example
of such spurious reasoning is a Connecticut state statute that requires
school boards to provide students terminated from the normal instructional program with an appropriate alternate educational program.

While the Commission respects the good intentions that lie behind
such reasoning, it challenges its realism. Public education is neither
"free" nor is it an inherent right that can never be forfeited. It is a
privilege. Accenting this position, the United States Supreme Court, in
the case of *San Antonio School District* v. *Rodriguez*, noted, "Education,
of course, is not among the rights afforded explicit protection under
our Federal Constitution. Nor do we find any basis for saying it is im-
plicitly so protected." Public education should be a privilege, enjoyed
by those students who demonstrate the responsibility necessary to acquire an education. The past decade has overemphasized the rights of
students. What is needed now is a concomitant thrust to emphasize a
fourth R – responsibility.[12] The courts are correct in determining that
student rights do not stop at the schoolhouse doors, but neither do the
responsibilities of students.

Some schools are becoming armed camps in their efforts to cope
with student crime and vandalism. The Commission looks with
dismay on many of these "solutions." Guard dogs, weapon detectors,
armed guards, and billy clubs are suitable for a prison or a combat
zone, but they contribute negatively to the educational setting. A more
viable alternative, in the Commission's view, is strong and effective
school management, particularly by school principals.

As a first step in this direction, the National Commission on Youth
recommends that school principals be given additional authority by
school boards and more legal backing by the courts to establish a tone
or an atmosphere in the school that will not tolerate acts of crime,

violence, and vandalism. Principals must establish this tone with policies that are fair, firm, and consistent. Humaneness is not to be confused with weakness. The severity of the punishment meted out for offenses is equally as important a deterrent as the swiftness and the certainty of punishment.

All of this constitutes a first step in the direction of restoring a measure of order to the public school system. Education, not survival, must once again become the primary task of public education.

The Juvenile Justice System

It is entirely possible that we are witnessing the demise of the traditional juvenile justice system. If so, it is long overdue. Consider the following example by way of illustration: the typical juvenile court refers a youth who assaults an elderly person to adult court, where he usually receives a probated sentence, while a youth who shoplifts or runs away from home might be given an indeterminate sentence.

From an analysis of juvenile-court versus adult-court sentences, although characterized by wide regional variations, the evidence suggests a much more lenient approach to youth than to adults for the same crimes. The failure of the courts generally in the prevention and punishment of crime suggests that leniency with offenders encourages disregard for the law. A serious need is a court system in which prompt hearing and the certainty of punishment are well-established practices and recognized as such by the public. To this must be coupled a thorough legislative and judicial overhaul of the relation of the severity of punishment to the severity of the criminal act. The changes in lifestyles made possible by technology and science in the last twenty-five years have rendered some sections of our penal code obsolete. New forms of crime are committed and old forms are passé.

While there must be firmness for youth in the judicial process, there must also be understanding. Juvenile judges should function as advocates for youth. As advocates, judges must demand greater accountability from key personnel in the rehabilitative process – teachers, probation officers, and social workers. Some enlightened juvenile judges are presently functioning in the courts as youth advocates. The National Commission on Youth applauds these efforts, viewing them as positive steps to reduce the present high levels of recidivism.

The Case of Status Offenders

Anyone who has ever been young probably has committed a delinquent act. Under various state laws, youth can be judged delinquent for the following actions: curfew violations, loitering, trying to marry, and running away from home. Adults cannot commit these offenses. These are "crimes" only young people commit. Since they are contingent on the age of the offender, they are labeled status offenses.

The National Commission on Youth defines a *status offense* as behavior that brings a juvenile to the attention of law enforcement agencies or related juvenile justice agencies but that would not be considered criminal if committed by an adult. Approximately 600,000 youth are arrested each year and placed in secure detention awaiting adjudication proceedings. More than one-third of those arrested are classified as status offenders.

How does one explain the development of this legal distinction? Around 1960, the notion came into vogue that certain types of behavior, then labeled delinquent, should be considered separately, namely, as a status offense. Thereafter, states began to label status offenders as PINS (Persons in Need of Supervision), CHINS (Children in Need of Supervision), MINS (Minors in Need of Supervision), or JINS (Juveniles in Need of Supervision). The hope was to eliminate stigmatizing youth as delinquents and to develop innovative alternatives for the juvenile court that would be more appropriate to the particular needs and circumstances of adjudicated youth.

These laudable aims have not been met. Neither has the stigma of delinquency been removed. Moreover, in many states status offenders are sent to detention centers or training schools where they frequently associate with convicted young criminals or hard-core delinquents. Such associations invariably have the effect of transforming an irascible youth into a hardened criminal.

Juvenile courts project a rhetoric of benevolency. In reality, however, they operate in harsher fashion than the regular courts. Only one-fourth of the population of juvenile training schools is incarcerated for serious offenses.[13] The remaining portion is imprisoned mostly for misdemeanors and status offenses. What are these facts saying? Juvenile courts tend to be more punitive toward noncriminal behavior.

Status offenders, as a class, are the forgotten children of the civil rights movement. They have not benefited significantly from the push for the rights of youth, set in motion by the *Gault* decision in 1967. Status offenders continue to rely on the all-too-whimsical discretion of judges. In some states they continue to be deprived of the right to be represented by counsel or protected from self-incrimination or double jeopardy, despite the fact that the Supreme Court has ruled that youth are entitled to these safeguards.

Several Commissioners believe that consideration should be given to the abolition of the juvenile-court system as a step toward clarifying the penalty-reward system of an urban society as it applies to youth and adults. There is great confusion about personal rights – where they end and where personal responsibilities and restraints begin. The concept of status offender for youth is one glaring example of this confusion.

As a first step in extending civil rights to youth designated as status offenders, the National Commission on Youth recommends that the jurisdiction of the juvenile-court system be limited only to those acts that if committed by an adult would constitute a crime, and to dependent and neglect statutes, which would allow the courts to intervene for the protection of the health and the welfare of youth.

Youth on the Run

Perhaps the cruelest laws are those designating runaway youth as status offenders. The philosophy that a minor's place is in the home is totally enforced by existing status-offender laws. This presumption persists regardless of the situation existing in the home. In some cases, it is more prudent to run than to stay.

Existing statutes and court decisions regarding the legal status of runaways are vague and contradictory, and vary from state to state. As recipients of such treatment from the law, runaway youth tend to view themselves as wanted criminals. They soon realize that they have no place to go, no means of receiving needed medical attention, no way of earning a living, and no hope for the future. Is it any wonder, then, that youth on the run are fair prey for unscrupulous adults who entrap them into prostitution, drug peddling, and other sordid forms of criminal activity?

What makes youth run? Internal emotions and external realities are equally important. Fear and depression vie for dominance in the minds of runaways. Oftentimes, runaways have an active fantasy life to compensate for severe inner tensions. "Growing up is like walking through a forest," explains Sarona Soughers, a high school senior in Melbourne, Florida. "You can't go around it," she adds, "you have to go through it." But for hundreds of thousands of American youth, the forest maze proves to be too formidable, causing them to flee to what they perceive to be less hostile environments.

An extremely high percentage of youth who run away reveal that they are victims of robbery, sexual and physical abuse, and other criminal acts. Yet, as badly as they need aid, the majority of runaways do not seek help for a variety of reasons: some are unaware of the availability of help; some have a sense of being stigmatized by the use of available services; some are fearful of being arrested as status offenders and returned home; and some feel helpless against the barriers to establishing their eligibility for treatment or assistance.

In view of these circumstances, the National Commission on Youth recommends that the act of running away be decriminalized as a status offense. It must be removed from the jurisdiction of the police and handled as a social and family-oriented problem. Elasticity must be injected into existing laws so that youth who leave home have the opportunity for reputable medical care, a decent place to live, a legitimate means of support, and continued education.

The Commission recommends further that a model statute be drawn up by the federal government and adopted by all states that safeguards the rights of the runaway and parental rights, that authorizes duly licensed physicians to provide medical care to minors under clearly defined circumstances, and that holds the physician blameless, both criminally and civilly, except for cases of negligence.[14]

The Juvenile Justice and Delinquency Prevention Act of 1974

The time has come for a new approach to juvenile justice. As long as we tolerate a system that turns delinquents, status offenders, and runaways into criminals, youth crime rates will continue at their present record-breaking levels.

The only thing the present juvenile justice system does that is unique is to lock youth up. The system does not provide any of the basic human services youth so desperately need. There is no such thing as correctional good health or good education or good counseling or good job training. Detentional budgets customarily allocate between 90 and 95 percent of their resources for custodial services, not for basic human services.

Prior to the passage of the Juvenile Justice and Delinquency Prevention Act of 1974, Congress addressed the problem of youth crime and delinquency through assorted pieces of legislation. Most of the funding was for rehabilitation programs for adjudicated delinquents rather than for programs designed to prevent delinquency. However, a growing body of evidence indicates that early identification and diversion toward alternatives to the juvenile justice system significantly reduce the rate of recidivism.

The Juvenile Justice and Delinquency Prevention Act gives priority to several specified areas. Briefly, these may be stated as follows: diversion, deinstitutionalization, and separation of juveniles from adult offenders. Special emphasis is placed on the prevention and control of juvenile delinquency. In short, the spirit of the new law rests on the adage that an ounce of prevention is worth more than a pound of cure. To do this, the following framework has been set up.

1. An Office of Juvenile Justice and Delinquency Prevention in the Law Enforcement Assistance Administration (LEAA) provides leadership and assistance for a wide array of federal juvenile justice programs.
2. A National Advisory Committee on Juvenile Justice and Delinquency Prevention advises the LEAA on federal programs.
3. Block grants are provided to state and local governments, and public and private agencies, including courts, to develop programs that emphasize the prevention of delinquency, diversion from the juvenile justice system, and the development of community-based alternatives to the traditional forms of incarceration.
4. The act provides that status offenders shall not be placed in detention or correctional facilities and that juveniles should not be incarcerated with adults.
5. The measure creates a National Institute for Juvenile Justice and Delinquency Prevention to serve as a clearinghouse and as a research, development, and dissemination center for juvenile justice programs.
6. The law includes a Runaway Youth Act, which permits local communities to establish temporary shelter/care facilities for runaway youth.

The act is not a panacea. It represents a beginning rather than an ending of efforts to cope with the problems of youth crime and delinquency.

Striking Out in New Directions: Some Key Issues

Crime and delinquency cannot be legislated out of existence any more than morality can be legislated into existence. The solution, like the problem, is complex.

It appears to the National Commission on Youth that there are inherent dangers in overestimating the capabilities of the helping professions to ameliorate youth crime and delinquency. Massive injections of social services do not necessarily change overall youth crime problems. Problems invariably arise whenever "the net is widened," thereby bringing more persons under social control through the use of less stringent sanctions. Whenever there is movement away from formal sanctions to less formal controls, there tends to be a subtle loss of procedural safeguards in the process.

The juvenile justice system can work, but it must be reconstituted along new lines. The key is to differentiate within the existing system by establishing gradations of responsibility. The Commission recommends that greater effort be made to differentiate in the various facets of the juvenile justice system.

Differentiated Sanctions. Presently there is a movement spearheaded by the Juvenile Justice Standards Project to differentiate among all the categories of youth crime and delinquency. The project goes so far as to say that a juvenile judge has the prescience to know just how much residential and nonresidential treatment is needed by an adjudicated youth. The National Commission on Youth views this as an impossible task and an imprudent remedy.

A more prudent approach would be a differentiated sanction that separates serious crimes from less serious forms of crime. Stronger sanctions should be applied to serious crimes, but an element of flexibility must be retained in sanctions for less serious crimes. In these instances, intermediate sentences should be meted out in order to vary the kind of flow of services that youthful offenders are subjected to in the rehabilitative process.[15] In such cases, the least restrictive alternative should be the chief criteria for intervention in the lives of youthful offenders and their families.

Differentiated Youth Needs. The ethos of most juvenile justice agencies is social work. While ethos may be necessary, it is most certainly not sufficient by itself. Pathos is also necessary in an equal degree.

The National Commission on Youth believes that it is also crucial to differentiate among the needs of youth on an educational basis, not strictly on a social basis.

It must be recognized that every young person's problems cannot be dealt with adequately by group therapy three times a week. This may be necessary, but at some point effective rehabilitation must take on an educative dimension. Most adjudicated youth do not suffer from serious emotional problems, but nearly all have serious educational deficiencies. Yet, in many detention centers and training schools, educational programs have a low priority, are ineffective, or simply do not exist.

Differentiated Services. One of the key factors in any system of juvenile justice is the concept of scale. The quality of service of any rehabilitative institution is determined by its size. The larger the institution, the greater the chances are of a counterculture developing within the institution.

The chief operating criterion for any rehabilitative institution should be the least restrictive, the least detrimental alternative. Secure institutions must be maintained for serious offenders, but the major thrust of programs should be to funnel youth back into the community setting on a differentiated basis.

There is no specific ideology that maintains that every adjudicated youth can be cared for most effectively in the community. Instead, the ideology is determined by the following realities: there are too many large institutions, large institutions are conducive to recidivism, and too many adjudicated youth, particularly status offenders, are inappropriately placed in institutional settings when they could be cared for more effectively in the community.

Probation Services. Probation services for youthful offenders are a disaster. In most areas they operate on a principle best characterized as "phony diversion."[16] When a youth is arrested for the first time, after the juvenile court hearing is completed the probation officer simply says, "Go home." Nothing else happens. This pattern may be repeated five or six times. Finally, an exasperated judge says, "You've had it! You're going to jail."

If proper intervention had taken place, probation services could have referred youth to appropriate community settings. For example, youthful offenders could be made to render some form of community service or be placed in an appropriate educational setting or be made to render restitution by some form of payment.

Federal Funding Patterns. Under Section 408 of the Social Security Act, states are granted formula reimbursement only for youth who are placed in private residential care. As a result, youth services often tend to develop along the lines of the reimbursement formulas.

The implications of this are disturbing to the Commission. Frequently, when the juvenile court has before it a decision of whether to leave an adjudicated youth at home and try to build some services into the family structure in order to keep that structure intact, it finds that these services are available only outside the home in some form of residential care. Thus the court is forced, time after time, to remove youthful offenders from the home and place them in residential care.

Regulation of Voluntary Agencies. While the National Commission on Youth recognizes that many voluntary agencies are providing yeoman service for adjudicated youth, it is concerned over a growing tendency by voluntary agencies to refuse services to youth with special problems. Many youth who are homosexuals or arsonists or have a history of being assaultive are turned away from voluntary agencies. Probation officers are often forced to shop around to place deviant youth in rehabilitation agencies. This shopping process can take weeks or even months, and, all the while, youth are not receiving badly needed services.

The National Commission on Youth is concerned that voluntary agencies are generally not accountable to any regulatory body, resulting in an uneven quality of services. It also must be recognized that in many states voluntary agencies incarcerate adjudicated youth for longer than justifiable periods of time, thereby ensuring the agency of an uninterrupted flow of government funding.

A Note of Caution

The juvenile justice system is best characterized at this point as caught between two ongoing reform movements – the deinstitutionalists and the incapacitators.[17] The former stress less use of institutions and any formal sanctions. Diversion, community-based treatment, and provision of services by noncoercive institutions are their goals. The latter, relying on deterrence and incapacitation theory, call for such measures as reducing the age of majority for criminal purposes and the mandatory waiver to adult court of older juveniles charged with serious crimes.

The present situation is most enlightening in that it reflects the public antipathy toward the problem of youth crime and delinquency. There are those who consider the system as too lenient toward youth crime. They see dangers in overestimating the capabilities of the helping professions, in "widening the net," and in the subtle erosion of procedural rights. Others maintain the system is overly severe and unjust to youth, especially those classified as status offenders. They sense dangers in indiscriminate incarceration and the loss of liberty for serious and nonserious offenders alike together with unrealistic crime-reduction expectations. At the moment, the deinstitutionalists are winning hands down in the search for alternatives to the present juvenile justice system.

The National Commission on Youth notes with a sense of alarm what might be euphemistically called "a local bite of the apple" philosophy. In many instances, it is possible for a youth to be apprehended six or seven times for criminal activities, yet continue to be treated as a first offender. Because of existing rules about sponging juvenile records, a youthful offender gets a new lease on life at each stage of the juvenile justice system – from the policeman on the beat, to the juvenile unit, to the court intake officer, to the juvenile judge, and finally to adult court, where he or she starts anew despite a lengthy record of arrests.

This philosophy gives youthful offenders the wrong message about the juvenile justice system. Youthful offenders fear what the juvenile court will do to them until they actually go to court. Then they learn their fears are wholly unfounded. The message comes through very clearly to youth – you will have many, many chances before anything will be done to you for your criminal activity.

Making Youth Accountable

The National Commission on Youth believes that it is inimical to the development of youth to convey to youthful offenders the idea that one does not have to be accountable for one's behavior because one is young. The message should go out loud and clear to youth that the fourth R in the basic competencies expected of all citizens is the concept of responsibility.

The National Commission on Youth does not favor increased incarceration for all youthful offenders. There is a vast difference, however, between accountability and incarceration. The Commission views restitution in the form of fines, payments to victims, and especially community service as viable alternatives to incarceration.

Finally, the Commission emphasizes that the effort to prevent youth crime and delinquency must be focused at early levels of intervention and diversion. Preventive efforts will have maximum impact on youth if such efforts are brought to bear on the natural settings in which they operate – the family, the neighborhood, the school setting, and, in general, on natural peer-group settings.

Notes

1. *FBI Uniform Crime Reports, Crime in the United States, 1975*, p. 188.

2. U.S. Department of Health, Education, and Welfare, *Juvenile Court Statistics, 1973* (U.S. Government Printing Office, Washington, D.C., 1975), p. 1.

3. Marvin E. Wolfgang, Robert M. Figlio, and Thorstein Sellin, *Delinquency in a Birth Cohort* (University of Chicago Press, Chicago, Ill., 1972), pp. 244-255.

4. Ibid., pp. 65-77.

5. M. Sherman, ed., *Long Range Thinking and Law Enforcement* (Hudson Institute, July 15, 1977), p. 53 of Chapter IV.

6. Paul C. Friday and Jerald Hage, "Youth Crime in Postindustrial Societies,"

Criminology, vol. 4, no. 3 (November 1976), p. 352.

7. George Gerbner and Larry Gross, "Living With Television: The Violence Profile," *Journal of Communications,* vol. 26, no. 2 (spring 1976), p. 176.

8. Grant H. Hendrick, "When Television is a School for Criminals," *T.V. Guide,* January 29, 1977.

9. Gerbner and Gross, "Living With Television," p. 187,

10. Remarks of Grace Baisinger, president, National PTA, at a meeting of the National Commission on Youth in Washington, D.C., April 28, 1978.

11. *Violent Schools—Safe Schools: The Safe School Study Report to the Congress,* executive summary, National Institute of Education, Department of Health, Education and Welfare, Washington, D.C., December, 1977.

12. B. Frank Brown, *Education for Responsible Citizenship,* National Task Force on Citizenship Education (McGraw-Hill Book Company, New York, N.Y., 1977), p. 5.

13. John M. Greacen, "Juvenile Delinquency and School Crime: Implications for School Administrators and Law Enforcement Personnel," 1976 /I/D/E/A/ Fellows Program.

14. Herbert W. Beaser, *Runaway Youth: From What to Where—The Legal Status of Runaway Children* (Educational Systems Corporation, Washington, D.C., April 1975), pp. 45-46.

15. Remarks by Peter B. Edelman, director, New York State Division for Youth, at a meeting of the National Commission on Youth in Miami, Fla., February 8, 1977.

16. Ibid.

17. Remarks by John M. Greacen, program director, Police Foundation, at a meeting of the National Commission on Youth in Washington, D.C., September 16, 1977.

7
HEALTH PROBLEMS OF YOUTH

Recommendation 18: Development of Improved Health-Care Delivery Systems. *The medical profession should take steps to develop improved health-care delivery systems for young people. Health-care services can be built into the organizational structure of community-based organizations, such as the Boys' Clubs, which serve large and diverse numbers of youth.*

Health programs that are participatory and continuing rather than passive and informational should be developed in secondary schools. The object of these programs should be to ensure that before leaving high school all young persons have an understanding of the nature of human reproduction and the dangers of smoking, drug abuse, and alcohol.

"Youth is too glorious to be wasted on the young," insisted George Bernard Shaw. Accepting the traditional wisdom of his time, Shaw believed that the second decade of life is a period of abundant health and a golden pause before the weighty burdens of adult existence fall on the shoulders of the young.

It is distressing to observe that for a substantial number of the young, adolescence is neither healthy nor golden. Instead, it is characterized by confusion, pain, and uncertainty. Glorious youth has become a period when social and environmental stress produce intolerable tensions. A stark indicator of the extreme effects of these pressures on adolescents is a 40 percent increase over the past five years in suicides among fifteen- to nineteen-year-olds and an increase of 30 percent in homicidal deaths. Nonwhite males are six times more likely to be the victims of homicide than white males. These are sobering and troubling statistics. They remind us that many of the social and physical environments antecedent to violent death cannot be changed by the victims.

Much of this chapter is an edited version of a presentation made to the National Commission on Youth by Charles U. Lowe, M.D., special assistant for Child Health Affairs, Office of the Assistant Secretary for Health, Department of Health, Education and Welfare, Washington, D.C., April 28, 1978.

A recent letter to the *New York Times* from a Harlem physician underscores the magnitude of the problem:

> [Urban youth] are among the most neglected of all the isolated and alienated inhabitants of [our cities] . . . they [constitute] a veritable army of tomorrow's adults who have few family ties, substandard medical and dental care, inadequate preparation for parenthood, and no goals. The toll they exact from the general population, both in financial and legal terms as well as in terms of conscience, is beyond count.

It would be erroneous to infer that young people in suburban and rural settings live in problem-free environments; in fact, their settings create special problems. They also share inequities in medical and health care experienced by their urban peers.

Defining the Health Needs of Youth

Health care and an array of ancillary services, such as sex counseling, legal assistance, recreation, and training in survival skills, are the core services to which young people need greater access. These services constitute the means to assist youth in the transition to the real world. Health services for the young in particular have received far too little attention. In treating the health needs of youth, three issues of paramount importance must be raised.

1. Why are adolescents special?
2. How can we best use our awareness of these special qualities and needs to shape the services we must provide for youth?
3. How can a community assess the range and mix of services needed by its young people?

The Developmental Process to Adulthood

How is adolescence special? Precious little agreement exists on this issue. Our personal perceptions are based on distant memories of our own adolescence, mellowed by the passage of time. Our present perception of youth, conditioned by personal contact, is often at odds with our memories. Finally, there are no clear-cut parameters of the age span of adolescence. Formal rites of passage to mark entry into and emergence from adolescence are notably absent in Western culture. Instead, adolescence is characterized by such actions as membership on school athletic squads, dating patterns, qualifying for a driver's license, and the legal purchase of alcoholic beverages. As a result, a variety of opinions exists about what adolescence is, when it starts, and when it ends. While its beginning is quite observable – a marked biological growth – its ending is far less obvious. We depend largely on social perceptions to identify the completion of adolescence.

Although the aging process follows a predictable sequence, the same cannot be said for the biological, social, and emotional transformations that characterize adolescence. These developmental processes are controlled by genetic signals and social opportunities. They are synchronized neither with each other nor with chronological age. A thirteen-year-old girl may mask her chronological identity with a sophisticated patina of social grace combined with biological maturity. The reverse is also commonplace; the tall, well-muscled seventeen-year-old athlete may find himself tongue-tied and awkward in a social milieu removed from the playing field.

We are aware of the discernible features of the maturation process. But chronological age alone is the determining factor in the expectations and the degree of emancipation permitted young people in the transition through adolescence. Consider young people's frustrations. They know they are capable of sexual intimacy, but because of their chronological ages, society says no. More troublesome to the adolescent is the expectation among adults that at the age of eighteen one acquires automatically the majority of adult attributes. Scant consideration is given to the notion that, because of the unevenness of the developmental process, an eighteen-year-old youth might be ill-prepared to conform to or to fulfill adult-role stereotypes.

For a variety of social, economic, cultural, or educational reasons, many Western nations have extended the transition period between childhood and the time when an individual enters the world of work. The implications of this policy of social determination of the parameters of adolescence are disturbing. It prolongs the adolescent's dependence on parents. The result is that full independence is achieved long after the attainment of social and biological maturation. This is in sharp contrast to the transition process in many developing nations. In these countries, childhood merges into adulthood with virtually no hiatus. This happens despite the fact that biological and psychological changes associated with adulthood have yet to manifest themselves. The changes frequently are completed long after the child is absorbed into the adult world.

What can one conclude from this cultural comparison? Either by design or by accident, Western society manipulates the length of adolescence for social and economic purposes. Such purposes are wholly unrelated to the natural developmental tasks confronting adolescents. Prolongation of the period of dependency not only inhibits the social maturation of the adolescent but also restrains parents from moving through the often befuddling passages of parenthood.

The sharp contrasts in traditions and ideologies, coupled with the interplay among social, biological, and chronological variables, make it difficult to generalize about the needs of adolescence. Biological development is invariate. But the social settings in which adolescence occurs and the expectations to which youth are subjected show remarkable differences both among and within cultures.

The Quest for Self-Identity

Despite the ambiguity in defining adolescence, an underlying theme permits constructive thinking and planning on the topic. Central to the growth of every adolescent is the unremitting search for self-identity in a constantly changing world. Four options exist to accomplish this end. The first is rebellion. This option fosters a simplistic view of the world and encourages a limited repertoire of social responses. The second option is simply giving up. This is a kind of emotional suicide and a totally passive reaction to social challenge. The third is adjustment, which suggests concessions – giving in rather than giving up. Inherent in this option is the liability that regret over important concessions made during adolescence may compromise the possibility of decisive action in adult life. The fourth option is coping. This option implies recognition of one's own needs, awareness of reality, and the use of the senses to appraise reality. Of these four options, coping is the most constructive and the most instructive way to achieve self-identity.

Helping Youth to Cope

Coping is a basic skill having lifelong applicability. Increased awareness and emphasis on the senses enable one to more readily discern reality in unfamiliar and ever-changing environments. If we foster the development of awareness, reliance on the senses, and reality testing as the main elements of coping, then health services can more effectively prepare adolescents for the transition to adult life.

What special characteristics do health services need to help youth develop a successful coping style? Service systems need to be designed on the basis of what is known presently about adolescent growth and development leading to the achievement of self-identity. Six features can be identified.

1. Because adolescents are undergoing rapid growth and changes that are destabilizing influences, the health-care system should be

made stable, consistent, and easily accessible. This eliminates one element of confusion in what is already a period of considerable turbulence for youth. Considering that adolescence is a period characterized by reality testing, the learning of new behaviors, and a quest for independence, it is a splendid opportunity to assist adolescents to develop new skills in the appropriate use of the health-care system.

2. Adolescents, in their search for self-identity and in response to maturational changes, are interested in and concerned about their bodies and appearance. This curiosity and concern are ideal motivations for learning. Opportunities must be created for young people to learn about their bodies, about what is happening to them emotionally, sexually, and physically, and about how to best care for themselves. It is imperative that this be a participatory and continuing experience rather than a passive, informational session. This will enable adolescents to exercise their decision-making skills and sharpen and strengthen their perceptions of alternative choices in personal health care.

3. Adolescents desire authoritative, but not authoritarian, adult relationships. Service providers can serve as personal role models and career models for the young. Service personnel need to be available to give young people opportunities to interact with them comfortably. The style in which health service providers present their views will determine the willingness of youth to respond. This precludes a "when-I-was-your-age" approach.

4. Adolescents need encouragement to strengthen their decision-making skills regarding personal health. It follows that health transactions with them need to be participatory. Health advice should include the discussion of alternatives and their consequences. This will foster a spirit of mutual responsibility for health-care decisions.

5. In addition to promoting increased self-responsibility, young people should be offered greater opportunity to exercise concern for family and community health. Health professionals, in response to increased demands for youth rights, should encourage adolescents to participate more fully in peer, family, and community health education. This function has been recognized by the World Health Organization in a 1977 report on the health needs of adolescents.

6. The growing sense of autonomy and individuality that characterizes adolescents must be nurtured. Maintaining the confidentiality of their perceived health needs and their health queries is a vital part of this. This poses a thorny dilemma: Under what circumstances is the young person treated independently, and at what point does one involve the family? Efforts should be made continually

to provide as much independence as the law permits or the individual can assume. Full emancipation from family suggests a degree of financial autonomy that most adolescents do not enjoy. Even if services are to be provided in a confidential manner, parental involvement cannot be avoided when payment for these services is at issue or when the service itself (such as major surgery) suggests an obvious need for parental involvement. The adolescent's family must also be viewed as a possible source of emotional support. The family is not the enemy. To the contrary, it can provide a vital part of the social structure within which self-identity can grow.

Two Immediate Concerns

Most schools presently educate youth to the dangers of alcohol and drug abuse. The Commission applauds these efforts and urges expansion of present programs as part of a comprehensive health program.

Two areas of particular concern to the members of the National Commission on Youth are the increase in teenage pregnancies and rise in cigarette smoking among the young.

Teenage Pregnancy. For most adults, the birth of a child is an occasion for joy and an investment in the future. For a teenage girl, particularly one who gives birth out of wedlock, the birth of a child is a tragic occasion, signifying a bleak future for mother and child alike.

One out of every ten teenage girls – approximately 1 million – are impregnated each year. In response to this fact, we have tried to ignore the problem, hoping it would disappear. It won't. In fact, the rate of teenage pregnancy is increasing. Pregnant teenagers can no longer be ignored by society. There are too many of them; their social and economic costs to society are too staggering to dismiss. Teenage pregnancy – the entry into parenthood of individuals who in many instances are barely beyond childhood themselves – is, from any viewpoint, a serious national problem.

Statistics underscore the magnitude of the problem.[1] Of the approximately 1 million girls who become pregnant each year, 400,000 are seventeen or under, 30,000 are fourteen or under. Of these 1 million girls, 600,000 have their babies. Although more than 235,000 of these babies are born out of wedlock, nine out of ten unmarried mothers keep their babies.

Consider the following consequences likely to befall an unwed teenage mother and her child.

A baby born to a teenage mother is considerably more likely to

die during the first year of life than a baby born to a woman
beyond the teenage years.

Eight out of ten women who become mothers by age seventeen
never complete high school.

The annual earnings of a woman who has her first child at fifteen or below are roughly 30 percent less than the earnings of
a woman who has her first child at age nineteen.

These are sobering personal statistics. But behind these personal
burdens are equally staggering financial burdens that society is forced
to assume.

Of all children born out of wedlock, 60 percent end up on welfare.

Half of the Aid to Families with Dependent Children (AFDC) –
some $4.6 billion in 1977 – goes to women who had their
first child as a teenager.

Adolescents have testified on numerous occasions that they need
and they want sex education. Several Gallup polls indicate that at least
70 percent of Americans believe that contraception should be taught
to youth in public schools. Despite these testimonials, there has not
been a commensurate rise in the extent to which states require even
the most basic instruction in human reproduction. Furthermore, in
those instances where operational programs exist, many are only
watered-down courses in the nomenclature of sexuality. Likewise,
although several government agencies have funded innovative programs, there is a pervasive, sometimes subtle neglect of sex and
family-life education in most government-sponsored programs.[2]

The reasons for this lack of initiative are easily discerned. Sex
education and family counseling is a political hot potato, a no-win
issue for politicians. Because sensitivities run so high on both sides of
the issue, those who hold public office prefer, if possible, to steer clear
of the issue. The end result is the institutionalization of ignorance.
While institutionalizing ignorance may temporarily solve the issue of
local politics, it serves to exacerbate the long-term effects of the problem. The final consequence is the development of costly social welfare
programs.

The National Commission on Youth is deeply concerned about the
results from the National Assessment of Educational Progress. It is
clear to Commission members that youth have an extremely limited
understanding of human reproduction. Only half of the nation's

seventeen-year-olds know that the embryo normally develops in the uterus; fewer than one-third know that the ovum is usually released fourteen days after female menstruation begins.[3] In light of these dismal results, the Commission strongly recommends that all young people have an understanding of the nature of human reproduction before leaving secondary school.

The Commission subscribes to the definition developed by the World Health Organization that sex education programs should be "far more broadly and imaginatively conceived to deal, not only with reproductive physiology, but with ethical issues." The ultimate goal of any program in sex education and family planning should be the development of mature individuals capable of making responsible decisions.

The Commission wishes to underscore the fact that the family is the primary educator of young people. The family unit is, properly, the first line of response to youth's needs for education in human sexuality. While nothing can ever truly replace each family's appropriate response to this need, schools can play an important role as a support system for familial values and teaching.

As sex educators, schools cannot and should not replace personal relationships that exist between parents and their progeny. Nor should schools usurp the important role that religious institutions can play as educators in human sexuality. But there are several compelling reasons why schools must accept a major responsibility in educating the young in human reproduction. Outside of the family, schools are the most pervasive influence in the lives of the young. Their impact continues for a considerable period of time. Most importantly, however, the public schools are organized and prepared to work with all youth – the washed and unwashed, the hard-to-reach and the not-so-hard-to-reach, the churched and the unchurched, and those who have confiding relationships with their parents as well as those who do not.

Effective sex education programs don't just happen. Program development does not occur in spectacular leaps. Instead, it inches forward, evolving over extended periods of time as mutual trust develops among school boards, parents, teachers, students, and the community in general. Moving forward also means having to move laterally at times and even stepping back for periods. Accommodation and compromise are essential to incorporate the feelings and the interests of the community into the curricular program.[4]

Teenage Smoking. Secondary schools can play an important role in educating youth to the hazards of cigarette smoking. Although the immediate effects of smoking are not as dramatic as teenage pregnancy, the long-term effects are potentially more destructive.

In 1964, the surgeon general of the U.S. Public Health Service issued the landmark report stating that cigarette smoking is detrimental to one's health. Since the report was issued, at least 30 million Americans have stopped smoking. But this trend is more than offset by the marked increase in smoking among youth, as borne out in the following statistics.

> Approximately 4,000 youth become cigarette smokers each day of the year.
> Among boys twelve to fourteen years of age, 5 percent smoke; among boys fifteen to sixteen years of age, 20 percent smoke; and among boys seventeen to eighteen years of age, 30 percent smoke.
> Boys formerly smoked at twice the rate of girls; now there is no longer a difference in the smoking rates between sexes.[5]

Joseph Califano, the former secretary of Health, Education and Welfare, became the bête noire of what is called the tobacco lobby—the alliance of tobacco growers, cigarette manufacturers, and advertising agencies whose aim is to maintain and expand cigarette smoking as an integral part of the American lifestyle.

Schools face a formidable foe in any attempt to educate youth to the dangers of smoking. The tobacco lobby spends a half-billion dollars annually on advertising designated to convince youth that smoking is glamorous, adult, and sexually attractive. The National Commission on Youth believes that society has a responsibility, through the schools, to educate youth to the dangers of cigarette smoking. The effort must be targeted squarely at youth, because the only certain way to stop the smoking habit is not to start.

Creating New Health Service Systems

It should be apparent from the above observations that the existing medical model is either ill constructed or inappropriately applied to respond adequately to adolescent needs. Are current health and medical practices too remote, institutionalized, and inflexible to assume new forms and procedures to better serve adolescents? It is not necessary to build a special service-delivery system for adolescents. Thought should be given, however, to developing both a new kind of provider and to examining the underlying philosophy that serves as a rationale for developing and providing health services. Were this to happen, significant changes would occur in the following service components: the range and mix of services, the payment system, and the training of those who serve adolescents. Such changes would affect the degree to which adolescents are involved in the planning, design, delivery, and evaluation of health services.

The creation of wholly new systems for adolescent health care is unnecessary. The key is to tap into existent systems. Individual states, local communities, and existing agencies and organizations can assess specific health problems and serve as indicators of unmet needs. They have in hand data such as vital statistics, program reports, and school health records. Most possess aggregated data that identify such individual and community problems as delinquency, youth crime, and runaways, as well as suicide, accident, and homicide rates among the young. But doing this will reveal more than unmet health needs. Such an accounting will reveal unsafe streets and schools, schools that offer no challenge, foreclosed employment opportunities, decaying neighborhoods, and limited or nonexistent recreational alternatives—the litany is endless. These are precisely the circumstances that generate a substantial portion of what eventually become adolescent health problems.

Solutions to problems that result from poverty and from physical and environmental stress will require enormous expenditures of imagination, energy, and money. Presently, we lack national guidelines to arrive at solutions. Although such uncertainties suggest caution, they do not excuse inaction. Sufficient empirical data exist to draft a preliminary blueprint for adolescent health services. Field studies are needed, however, to verify the data. To know more about the health status and health needs of adolescents, ask them directly.

A Preliminary Blueprint for Adolescent Health Services

The Robert Wood Johnson Foundation has been investigating models for improving the accessibility and the quality of primary medical services for adolescents who are inadequately served by present delivery systems. Too old for the pediatrician and too young for the internist, adolescents tend to fall between the cracks in the present systems of health care. The peculiar health-related needs of adolescents are not served best simply through the intervention of a physician. Instead, these needs appear to be met most effectively through a variety of health education programs.

The Johnson Foundation believes that voluntary organizations can play a role in more effectively meeting the health needs of young people. Because these organizations relate in a significant manner to large numbers of youth, they may be able to provide young people with the knowledge and the skills to make more effective utilization of health services.[6]

Operating on this assumption, the Johnson Foundation has embarked on a major effort involving three of the country's major youth organizations – the Boy Scouts of America, the Boys' Clubs of America, and the national 4-H organization. The organizational choice is significant for several reasons. First, the combined membership of the organizations is comprehensive, representing 12 million youth between the ages of eight and nineteen. Second, the organizations' focuses are complementary: the Boy Scouts are very strong in suburban areas, the 4-H in rural areas, and the Boys' Clubs in the inner cities.

Boy Scouts of America. The primary thrust of this program is to revise and update numerous scouting manuals and related publications. All existing publications were reviewed for the purpose of updating health-related information in six basic areas: physical fitness and exercise; nutrition and diet; human physiology; family life and emotional health; utilization of community health resources; and safety and first aid. Simultaneously, the Scouts are reviewing their leadership training procedures in order to develop more effective techniques to disseminate this health information.

4-H Organization. Whereas the Boy Scouts are a highly structured hierarchial organization, 4-H stresses the autonomy of local units. Their educational philosophy is based on the premise that one learns by doing.

Under the terms of the Johnson Foundation grant, 4-H is providing support to local units in two states to develop innovative approaches to health education, based on a "learning by doing" approach. Eventually, 4-H hopes to develop a set of health education guidelines based on these local experiences. Ultimately, the guidelines will be disseminated on a national basis throughout the organization, with local clubs adapting them to their own particular local needs.

Boys' Clubs of America. Five Boys' Clubs across the country are participating in this project. This is the most ambitious design of the three because, in addition to the health education program, there is also a health service component. The health service component consists of three parts:

1. A physical examination for each member
2. A health advocate responsible for follow-up treatment on any

health problem disclosed in the preliminary examination
3. Arrangements for treatment services that are made with local
    health-care providers, including physicians, public health
    clinics, and hospital outpatient departments

Each club is developing its own approach to health education programs, focusing on obvious areas of concern to male adolescents:
drugs, alcohol, smoking, venereal disease, immunization, nutrition,
and first aid and safety.

Out of the experiences of these five clubs, the Boys' Clubs expect to
develop a set of guidelines for national dissemination. It is hoped that
these guidelines can encourage local units to move more actively to
meet their members' health needs.

The National Commission on Youth commends these initiatives and
sees the possibility of important ancillary effects developing from this
prototype effort. For example, in many parts of the country such
voluntary organizations and agencies as 4-H work closely with the
schools. Such combined efforts could conceivably "widen the net,"
thereby reducing the possibility that young people will continue to
slip through cracks in the present health-care system.

Some Concluding Observations

What conclusions can be drawn from the above observations?

• We must recognize that adolescence is a special time of life. It is
singularly critical in determining adult behavior and health status. It
is most certainly the principal time when young people develop the
skills they need to make a successful transition to the world of adults.
Fundamental to this transition is the acquisition of techniques for
coping, for making well-informed decisions, and for acquiring a
realistic self-image.

• We have more than sufficient empirical data confirming that ill
health is far more common among adolescents than traditional
wisdom suggests. But the causes of illness, be they biological or social
in origin, carry with them a strong behavioral component that must be
recognized.

• The affective components of adolescent ill health are only rarely
or intermittently addressed within current health delivery systems.
Many adolescent health problems simply do not lend themselves to effective treatment within the current medical model.

• It follows logically that the current delivery system of services
must be modified to recognize not only the unique nature of adoles-

cence but also the interrelatedness of social, biological, and emotional problems. A first and critical step in achieving this goal is to change our thinking and actions regarding the content of and processes used to plan and deliver services to this group.

• It must be acknowledged that the social forces burdening young people are multiple and complex. Provision of health services alone will not solve these complex issues. To take the steps outlined above constitutes a significant beginning. Our existing knowledge, skills, and professional experience, coupled with the considerable energy and insight of adolescents, are sufficient to complete the task.

The most urgent needs at this point are leadership and commitment.

Notes

1. Julius Richmond, M.D., *Adolescent Pregnancy*, Hearing before the Subcommittee on Select Education of the Committee on Education and Labor, House of Representatives, July 24, 1978 (U.S. Government Printing Office, Washington, D.C., 1978), pp. 16-17.

2. Peter Scales, "Sex Education and the Role of the Federal Government," *Searching For Alternatives to Teenage Pregnancy*, National Organization for Non-Parents, Baltimore, Md., 1978, p. 18.

3. National Assessment of Educational Progress, *What Students Know and Can Do*, Education Commission of the States, Denver, Colo., 1977, p. 83.

4. George H. Thoms, "Community Involvement Key to Sex Education in Falls Church," *Searching For Alternatives to Teenage Pregnancy*, National Organization for Non-Parents, Baltimore, Md., 1978, p. 14.

5. Leonard S. Baker, "To Help Schools Combat Smoking," *American Education*, U.S. Department of Health, Education and Welfare, October 1978, vol. 14, no. 8, p. 19.

6. Remarks by Frank Jones, program officer, Robert Wood Johnson Foundation, to a meeting of the National Commission on Youth, Washington, D.C., April 28, 1978.

PART 3

ASSESSING YOUTH POLICY

8

YOUTH POLICY IN THE CITIES: A SELECTIVE ANALYSIS

Recommendation 19: Youth Transitional Planning Councils as Policymaking Bodies. *Mayors, acting as youth advocates, should designate and utilize youth transitional planning councils as mechanisms to develop youth policies and programs on the local level.*

Recommendation 20: Federal and State Guidelines to Local Communities. *Federal and state policy guidelines to local communities should be prescriptive, not restrictive, in character. The purpose of such guidelines should be to establish a nominal amount of monitoring of youth programs, to provide leadership, and to create incentives for organizations and individuals who serve youth on the local level.*

In recent years, society has been deluged with information concerning youth and the problems youth face in an increasingly urbanized society. Wading through the literature, which spans a wide spectrum of social and political thought, a person cannot help confronting the compelling questions, What does it all mean? Where does anyone begin to make sense out of the multitude of profound, profuse, and provocative words of wisdom?

The problems of urban youth are as complex as they are manifold. People tend to take a stereotyped view of the problems of urban youth. They picture the problems as those of poor, urban, minority, delinquent youth as if such youth were a homogeneous group. But youth under any circumstances are not a homogeneous group. Some need only a job; others need remedial services and support; still others desperately need medical care; and others, as a last resort, must be supported by the government, for they will always have difficulty finding and holding a job.

Surprisingly enough, there is a fairly clear-cut explanation, albeit oversimplified, to this complex situation. To begin with, there is an area of overlap or agreement that forms an undercurrent in the majority of youth-related writing and studies. The overriding common theme is that, first of all, there is a profound lack of opportunities for urban youth to engage in *meaningful* participation and involvement in society and, secondly, there is a lack of socially acceptable and gratifying relationships with a variety of adults.

One need not be an enlightened newspaper reader or news watcher to become aware of the patterns that emerge from these alarming trends. The media continually bombards us with countless statistics and graphic examples of the rising incidence of juvenile crime, violence, and vandalism.

Whatever the percentages, growing up and accepting adult responsibilities has become for many young people an increasingly difficult task. These trends tend to be exacerbated in the cities. It is here where media statistics are transformed into reality. Local officials contend with a daily diet of youth crime, vandalism, unemployment, and drug abuse.

Funding Local Programs

Any discussion on local youth programs inevitably ends with a big question: Where is the money coming from? It comes from a variety of sources, including state and local monies, federal funds, and assorted private sources.

Since 1973, the Comprehensive Employment and Training Act (CETA) has played a progressively larger role in funding youth programs at the local level. CETA represents a dramatic change. Traditional categorical grants have been abandoned in favor of block grants to cities acting as prime sponsors.[1] With the resultant emphasis on decategorization and decentralization, local governments now enjoy considerable latitude to shape programs in response to local needs. Assured of adequate levels of funding and freed from bureaucratic restraints, communities can experiment with youth programs that formerly were only dreams.

Four Model Programs

Staff members of the National Commission on Youth visited four city programs selected by the National League of Cities and the U.S. Conference of Mayors as outstanding programs for youth. Essentially these programs attempt to respond to youth needs and offer opportunities for socially acceptable participation in local communities and society at large. Two are federally funded through CETA, one is state funded, and the fourth operates primarily on city funds.

The types of experiences young people receive in these exemplary programs are of particular interest as models for the development of new youth initiatives. Also noteworthy are the variety of approaches these programs used in coordinating their services with other youth services in the city. The programs link schools with work places, the private sector with public resources, labor unions with youth agencies, supportive services with training in specific skill areas, and CETA dollars with state and local funds.

Boston, Massachusetts — Youth Activities Commission

Historic Boston represents a striking contrast of past and present. Wide, modern streets disappear into the crooked, narrow streets of colonial Boston, lined with boutiques, galleries, and quaint shops. Skyscrapers cast their shadows on streets and squares where Paul Revere and Samuel Adams once trod.

However, Boston, like all of the cities the Commission visited, is plagued with serious youth problems. Unemployment for youth reaches up toward the 60 percent mark in many areas. Juvenile crime and violence have risen dramatically. Drug and alcohol abuse among teenagers is rampant. The extent and severity of these problems and all their ramifications are staggering.

The Youth Activities Commission (YAC) was created in 1965 as one attempt to deal with the myriad of problems faced by youth in the city of Boston. By legislative mandate, the major task of the YAC is to establish and to carry on programs designed to reduce or prevent delinquency and to improve the health and welfare of juveniles in need of guidance, recreation, counseling, education, placement, or social or cultural development. The target population is young persons from the age of seven to seventeen.

The Youth Activities Commission operates under four sources of funding. (Youth programs tend to come and go, often with little notice or recognition. It is important to note that a key positive factor that tends to increase the durability and longevity of youth service agencies and programs is diverse sources of funding. While the Youth Activities Commission is funded from a variety of sources, its fourteen-year existence has been basically dependent on funds from city hall.) The primary flow of dollars comes from a million-dollar budget from the city of Boston. YAC has also recently obtained a large diversion grant from the Law Enforcement Assistance Administration (LEAA) to develop programs aimed at diverting first- and second-time offenders from the court system. In addition, the Commission receives a welfare grant from the state of Massachusetts to offer counseling to welfare recipients and their families. Though not the direct administrating agency, YAC is charged with monitoring and evaluating CETA youth manpower programs. Also, out of a total staff of 250 workers, approximately 125 staff members are on the CETA payroll.

Boston is a city with a tradition of strong ethnic ties. The division among neighborhoods and communities along ethnic and cultural lines is prominent. Reflecting Boston's historical antecedents and ethnic diversity, the Youth Activities Commission operates and administers programs through twelve neighborhood resource centers, virtually covering the city. The centers are semiautonomous. Their goal is to develop and to implement programs commensurate with the needs of their respective neighborhoods and clientele.

YAC bases its operation on the area youth-work concept. Each resource center is composed of a director, a number of supervisors, case managers, police liaison workers, and a series of social workers who either have street assignments (in which case they are called area youth workers) or assignments in the schools (where they are referred to as school workers).

The crux of YAC operations is the direct service personnel. Offering a wide range of services to their clients, they provide counseling, referral assistance, advocacy work, job placement, and tutoring. The key to the effectiveness of the program is the linkages and relationships youth workers have established with various community institutions.

Youth workers fill a pervasive gap. As in most large cities, school guidance counselors and court probation officers are overwhelmed by the sheer force of numbers. Youth workers are located in the schools, the courts, police stations, and on the streets. They are familiar with the problems young people face as well as with their needs. Workers can respond as a model or supplement for some need that is lacking—a counselor, a resource person, or simply a friend.

The director of the Allston-Brighton Center offers some interesting comments and insights.

> The problem, in my way of looking at it, is that we don't have enough true alternatives. There is nowhere for youth to go. We have got to find places, and that is basically what we do. We try to take the individual who has got a myriad of problems and deal with all these things—with all the fragments of his life—and put them together. But it is all for naught if we don't have anywhere for that youth to aim. He has got to have a goal. There has got to be some place where he can go. That is what the transition from childhood to adulthood is. There is no transition if there is no place for him to be an adult.

Intervention work in the schools became a reality with the advent of desegregation and the resultant busing issue. Youth Activities Commission workers were placed in the schools as negotiators between black and white students as well as mediators in crisis situations. The busing controversy has diminished appreciably, but the Youth Activities Commission has continued to maintain an active school involvement program.

The Youth Activities Commission also functions as a delinquency prevention organization. The aim is to reduce and control the amount of juvenile delinquency in the city of Boston. Historically, YAC has been an all-purpose agency offering services to all young people in Boston. Thousands of young people have benefited from the services provided by scores of youth workers and staff.

YAC administrators are faced with a critical dilemma. After years of providing services, the staff is *subjectively* convinced that they are providing much-needed services and that they operate an efficient, effective, and beneficial youth service-delivery system. On the other hand, they are held accountable for the funds they receive and must prove the positive value of continued existence. It is very difficult, however, to quantify and measure such value *objectively*. Unfortunately, during the Youth Activities Commission's existence, juvenile delinquency in Boston, as in other cities, has increased rather than diminished.

In order to work toward more realistic outcomes, have more of an impact on controlling the amount of juvenile delinquency in Boston, and justify future funding and existence, YAC has experienced a recent shift in priorities. While no youngster that requests services will be turned away, the current emphasis is toward dealing with first- and second-time offenders along with chronic offenders—the small minority of young people responsible for committing the majority of juvenile crimes.

It is believed that through this reorganization and focusing efforts on a specific youth population, the Youth Activities Commission will be able to maximize benefits and achieve greatest impact in reducing delinquency, given the agency's limited resources.

Although the target population of the Youth Activities Commission has become less broad, the goals of the youth workers are no less difficult to achieve and the situations they are faced with no less complex. As the YAC executive director explains it, "What we are trying to do here is provide consistent, positive support for young people that will enable them to deal with their personal and family needs, with education, and employment. If we can handle these three things, we will have accomplished a major miracle."

Baltimore, Maryland – Harbor City Learning

What do you do with students who are turned off by traditional high school or have dropped out? Baltimore, Maryland, thinks it has the answer. It is called Harbor City Learning (HCL).

Harbor City Learning grew out of the fact that in Baltimore, as in many other cities, the dropout rate is alarming. As many students drop out of the Baltimore City School System as graduate – approximately 8,200 per year. An additional 40,000 youth are classified as chronic truants. HCL is an alternative educational model that is getting many dropouts back into school and preventing many other students from quitting.

Harbor City Learning was initiated by the Mayor's Office of Manpower Services, the CETA prime sponsor in the Baltimore area. HCL planners faced an inital philosophical decision: whether to run the program solely through the mayor's office or jointly with the school system. They chose the latter, and HCL is a successful example of *cooperation* and *coordination* of resources between two separate institutions offering a unique array of services to hundreds of young people in Baltimore.

The school system provides a principal, assistant principal, and a score of teachers. Administrators, coordinators, and support staff are funded through the mayor's office.

The program administrator explains that one of the first things Harbor City Learning planners looked at before developing the model was the fundamental question of why young people drop out of school:

> We found out that youth drop out of school for two reasons: One, school doesn't mean anything to them, for there is no relevancy attached to it. What they are doing in school has no relevancy to the world of work or just growing up. Two, they need money. So, there is an economic reason and there is a relevancy issue in there. We developed a model around both of those things in which we try to tie the academic part to the work experience.

Consequently, Harbor City Learning has two major dimensions. There is an educational component in which students spend part of their time in a nontraditional academic setting that leads either toward a general equivalency diploma (GED) or high school diploma. The second dimension is a work experience component in which students spend two weeks out of a month in a subsidized work experience selected in conjunction with their individual interests.

The backbone of the program is four occupational clusters or mini-schools—health, communications and transportation, community services, and business. The cluster designations are significant. Based on current labor market projections, the clusters reflect the best estimates of where jobs will exist in the Baltimore of the future. Approximately 160 students are assigned to each cluster. Every two weeks, students move from the classroom into public-sector work sites in the city where students can sample jobs in their chosen clusters.

The city becomes the classroom, and there is no lack of diversity in work sites. Students can be found working in such areas as pediatrics wards, autopsy rooms, hospital pharmacies, offices, communication departments, day-care centers, and nursing homes. The response is positive. Since the program's inception, some 1,800 former dropouts have participated, with approximately 350 students receiving high school diplomas or GEDs.

The principal of Harbor City Learning emphasized that a key factor determining the success or failure of HCL is that work sites must be chosen carefully and adequate supervision provided.

> We must help the work sites in realizing that we are not sending them a finished product. When we take a sixteen-year-old dropout and send him to your particular place, you are not getting an experienced mechanic; you are getting a young person who has *some* idea what he wants to do, but he does not know *exactly* what he wants to do. Thus, it is a looking process. We should have enough jobs so they can move around in many different areas of work.

Harbor City students are provided with a relevant curriculum meshing academic learning with real-life, hands-on situations. They gain exposure to the world of work and employers' expectations. Unlike scores of young people throughout the country, most have concrete labor market experiences as well as opportunities for career and vocational exploration when they graduate.

The approach that the planners of Harbor City Learning have taken is to create a program with simple, clear-cut goals and objectives, developing expertise in a narrowly defined area. The original goal was to retain school dropouts and potential dropouts. As the program has evolved, however, a flexible model has been maintained. Rather than constantly creating new programs with new administrative structures, if a program is effective it is supplemented. The expansion is incremental.

Since it started, Harbor City Learning has incorporated an in-school model and added two additional clusters—human services in the arts, and vocational careers. This made 750 more slots available. Work opportunities are identified for students in fields related to their studies and interests. Students in the in-school component work part-time earning minimum wages. The majority are vocational students who work in the areas of carpentry, plumbing, auto repairs, painting, and interior decorating. Other students work in positions where they receive training in the visual and performing arts.

One of the more successful projects has been housing rehabilitation where students work with professional help and guidance to renovate dilapidated housing. They provide a community service while acquiring skills supplementing their classroom learning.

Responsibility to work is tied to attendance in school. Students can only work if they attend school. The results have been quite dramatic. Students who have missed over 70 days of school in past years are now absent on rare occasions.

In the last couple of years, Harbor City Learning has set up two centers for supportive services, recognizing that many dropouts face problems that prompted them to drop out in the first place.

One is a student resource center where students receive personal counseling, job information, and career guidance and begin to formulate plans for the future after graduation from Harbor City Learning. Another unique service is the Parent Infant Center, where children of HCL students learn as well. In the past, many students' attendance was sporadic because they had to attend to their children's day-care needs. Young parents receive training in child rearing and HCL students are able to participate with full-time teachers in working with and designing activities for the children.

Unfortunately, HCL is faced with a formidable obstacle. In the words of the principal, "We have a tremendous population out there that needs this particular service that we offer. What hurts me, what causes me to boil, is that the need is so great but we can only deal with so few. So many young people fall between the cracks and we lose them."

For many young people in Baltimore, Harbor City Learning is the end of the road—their last option. One former dropout in the business cluster succinctly states this outlook: "I figure if you're not going to make it in Harbor City, you won't make it in any other place. Because you're getting paid a little bit of money for working, and getting an education, too."

Portland, Oregon—Youth Services Division

The city of Portland, through its Youth Services Division, operates a unique and comprehensive youth service delivery system that attempts to influence the lives of the city's youth through two major components. The division director explains the organizational setup:

> Our program is pretty much set up into two areas. One is in terms of Youth Employment and all that is involved with this, and the other is the Youth Service Centers. Youth Service Centers are primarily diversion centers. In addition to that, inside the centers is our area manager. The area manager is the person responsible for the employment component of each geographical area. So between those two service delivery mechanisms, we can relatively deal with most of the problems youth are facing.

The career training offices are located within the offices of the youth service centers in order to consolidate resources under one roof and avoid fragmentation of services.

In many instances, Portland's system is similar to the previous programs mentioned. As in Boston, youth service centers are set up in various areas of the city responding to different needs of local neighborhoods and communities. These centers also offer direct and referral assistance to young people and their families. The centers are concerned with delinquency prevention and function as a community-based resource and alternative to the juvenile justice system.

Portland's Career Training Office, like Baltimore's, is able to offer subsidized work experience to numerous young people through a number of projects. For many of the young people, it is their first experience in the "world of work." The purpose of the program is to increase the employability of participants through on-the-job training, education, skill training, and supportive services.

There are several interesting aspects unique to Portland's youth program. One is the linkage between the Youth Services Division and the city school system. The focal point of this relationship is the presence of work experience coordinators in the schools. Each high school has a work experience coordinator, paid by the school system, to develop work experience and training-type activities for that school. Area managers work with the coordinators to offer services to in-school youth, to encourage students to remain in school. In essence, the work experience coordinator serves as a liaison between the CETA-funded Youth Services Division and the city school system.

A division career training coordinator outlines the benefits of this approach:

> This has the advantage of our system being able to serve youth through a

system that is internal to the school. One very definite benefit is that we do not have to pay the work experience coordinators in each one of those high schools. In addition, the young person that the high school work experience coordinator serves becomes part of the school program. He can earn credit for working. We couldn't give credit because we are not part of the school system.

Each young person who participates in the work experience program works in conjunction with the area manager to create a career development plan. The plan identifies all training and support service needs and outlines all activities and services for the youth, including expected accomplishments and time lines. This defines the responsibilities of the youth and the program. There are periodic evaluations to determine how far the young person has proceeded in relation to the plan.

One of the serious drawbacks of subsidized work experience programs is that, even though young people receive valuable experience and develop work habits, when they complete the program often there are no jobs available, no opportunities to utilize newly formed skills.

The Youth Services Division has recently initiated a small but very successful program to deal with this situation. If a youngster has work experience and is prepared and mature, he or she might be placed in on-the-job training in the private sector. In this program, a private employer hires the young person and the Youth Services Division reimburses the employer for a percentage of the cost. This covers the additional cost an employer would have to pay for training. This provides private industry with the opportunity to train youth for jobs in skill areas where critical shortages of labor exist. Training is provided on the job site by the sponsoring business. The young workers are treated as employees of the training organization and are on the organization's payroll. If the new employee is successful and establishes a good work record during the six-month training period, it is expected that he or she will then be hired as a full-time employee. Each participant's chances for success are enhanced by support provided through the staff of the individual career training office.

Olympia, Washington—Program for Local Service

All of the programs mentioned previously are geared toward the low-income, disadvantaged young person. The most widely heard complaint administrators have to deal with is from parents or from young people themselves who request and need the services offered but are turned away because their family income falls somewhere above the cutoff point for eligibility. This is not a problem with the Program for Local Service located in the state of Washington.

Program for Local Service (PLS) is designed so that every young person who applies has an equal opportunity to become a volunteer. There are no educational requirements, and volunteers are not required to come from any particular income group or possess a particular skill.

Originally a pilot project funded by the ACTION agency in 1973, PLS is now solely supported by the state of Washington. As previously indicated in Chapter 3, it is a small-scale but very successful example of a National Youth Service.

The PLS director indicates that the uniqueness and keynote of the program stems from its emphasis on service: "The service model we are into, while we focus on the participant very much, says that for this program to be viable and valuable there has to be a benefit to the community and to people in need in the community. We are saying, participants in the program have something valuable to give – and we have proven that."

In very simple terms, the success of the program is derived from the fact that there are enormous unmet human, social, and environmental needs in communities throughout the country. In the PLS model, local communities are surveyed and a catalog of volunteer opportunities is developed. The goal of volunteer recruitment is to offer every young person between eighteen and twenty-five an equal opportunity to serve the community in the areas where the program is operating.

Contrary to other work-related programs, applicants are not placed in positions. Rather, potential volunteers attend an orientation session in which they learn about the program and are assisted by "matchmakers" or "brokers" in setting up appointments with local sponsoring agencies of their choosing.

Potential volunteers and sponsors then begin a process of interviewing, seeking to find mutually agreeable activities. At the end of this process, volunteers and sponsors negotiate a memorandum of agreement outlining the terms of a contract for the volunteer's year of service. The agreement is based equally on the participant's skills and interests and the needs of the sponsoring agency.

The Program for Local Service utilizes the relatively new concept of the stipended volunteer. The emergence of this type of program grew out of the realization afforded from the Peace Corps experience that volunteerism had been previously restricted to those who could afford to volunteer, mainly middle- to upper-class women. Second came the realization that many communities and agencies have a tremendous need for the services that volunteers can provide.

PLS has been in existence for five years and has compiled some impressive results. About 1,500 participants have served, meeting a range of community needs. As PLS volunteers, they serve for one year full-time and manage to live on less than $50 per week. The program has emphasized the viability of a system of local service delivery, training, programming, and supervision. All aspects of the program are carried out on a local community basis.

The common feature of PLS volunteers is that prior to joining, over seven out of ten were unemployed and looking for work. When surveyed three months after leaving the service, only 12.3 percent (a decrease of 60.2 percent) were unemployed and looking for work.

The total cost to maintain a volunteer in service for a year is less than $4,000, while the services performed by each volunteer average over $9,000.

Many of the sponsors said that the services being performed by the Program for Local Service volunteers were invaluable to their agency. Administrators normally receive about three times as many requests for volunteers as they can place.

Somewhat surprisingly, there is a high percentage of minority participation as well as a lower average income of the households of the PLS volunteers in comparison with the average in the state of Washington (see Table 8.1). This occurs although there is no specific income criteria for eligibility.

One PLS training coordinator is convinced that this is the best approach: "I think young people are saying, 'Give me a chance to prove myself. Don't give me a handout; don't label me as disadvantaged on lack of skills; give me a chance to prove myself.' And I think the model Program for Local Service says, 'Hey, young person—you have something to offer your community' and they want to do it."

Some Summary Observations

The four programs referred to in this chapter seek to respond to the needs of young people by offering support for and developing linkages between the various transitional institutions and by providing opportunities for young people to engage in responsible and desirable activities. Two incontrovertible facts stand out in all four programs: youth want to work if given a chance; and most of the people who staff the programs genuinely wish to help youth.

The programs cited represent four examples out of dozens of poten-

Table 8.1. Demographic Characteristics of Program for Local Service Enrollees

| | Racial Characteristics[a] | |
	Population (Percentage)	PLS Volunteers (Percentage)
Black	6.9	14.0
Spanish origin	2.0	0.6
Other nonwhite	5.3	5.6
White	85.8	79.8

Household Income of PLS Enrollees[b]
(1 year before enrollment)

Income	Percentage
$ 0– 1,000	10.7
1,000– 3,000	22.4
3,000– 4,000	10.7
4,000– 7,000	8.6
7,000–10,000	12.8
10,000–15,000	13.4
15,000– Over	13.1

Personal Income of PLS Enrollees[c]

Income	Before PLS (Percentage)	Following PLS (Percentage)
$ 0– 1,000	56.7	1.1
1,000– 2,000	11.1	2.1
2,000– 3,000	11.1	5.4
3,000– 4,000	6.7	7.6
4,000– 5,000	12.2	16.3
5,000– 6,000	2.2	19.8
7,000– 8,000	–	15.2
8,000– 9,000	–	17.4
9,000–10,000	–	12.0
10,000– Over	–	3.3

[a]Members of minority groups are participating at a greater rate than members of non-minority (white) groups. Blacks are represented at twice the frequency of whites compared to the respective proportions in the target population, the 18–25 age group.

[b]Average household income of families of PLS volunteers is $7,150. The average household income of families in the state is $12,900. PLS tends to attract lower-income applicants. Nevertheless, the participant group is a broad population cross-section comprised of volunteers from poor, middle, and upper income backgrounds.

[c]Prior to joining PLS, 97.8 percent of the PLS volunteers had an average personal income of less than $5,000, with 56.7 percent having an annual income of less than $1,000. Following their year with PLS, 67.7 percent of the PLS volunteers had an income of over $5,000.

Source: This information was assembled by the staff of the National Commission on Youth.

tial models for youth programs. However, there are a few important features common to these particular programs that will determine the success of any youth-serving program or agency.

Clear-Cut Goals and Objectives. Program administrators and staff must have a clear sense of just what it is they are trying to accomplish. They must then develop simple, comprehensible, and attainable goals, after which an effective implementation strategy can be developed.

Effective Supervision. It is of the utmost importance that effective supervision for both the staff and young people in the program be provided. Supervisory practices are most effective when based on low supervisor-client ratios. When possible, older youth with prior successful experience in the program should be hired as supervisors.

Community-Based Programming. The most effective programs are those that respond to local community and neighborhood needs and characteristics. Myriad social and institutional forces shape a young person's life. Staff must develop relationships with the various community institutions in order to coordinate resources and develop an effective approach toward dealing with young people.

Youth Participation. Very simply, without the active participation of youth in organizing the program, it is very difficult to structure and develop programs that are responsive to the young people they are trying to serve.

Careful Staff Selection. The director of the Portland program most appropriately phrases the key to staff selection: "You've got to really like kids. That is how we choose our staff. We choose people who genuinely love kids. When you do that, programs have a tendency to work."

Adequate Funding. Money is a reality but not a panacea. The distinction is subtle, yet crucial. No one would question that adequate funding is an absolute necessity. Money by itself, however, does not guarantee success. This is achieved only by the development of creative programs. Successful programs don't just spend money; rather, they utilize it in creative ways.

Evolving Youth Policy in the Cities

Establishing youth policy on the local level is no easy task. There are no magic formulas or sure-fire strategies. Ultimately, these must be forged in response to local needs and pressures. There are, however, as this chapter points out, some promising practices and programs that might well be adapted by cities. The potential of the successful programs presented for the development of youth policy on the local level is clear.

The Mayor

All too often, people expect local policy to be shaped from above and handed down intact to be digested by local officialdom. There are better places to start. A more logical starting point is the place where most local problems eventually come to be resolved – the mayor's office.

Youth, typically, have no power base in most communities. Consequently, the mayor or his equivalent must serve as an advocate or broker for the interests of youth. The National Commission on Youth recommends that mayors, acting in the capacity of youth advocates, utilize youth transitional planning councils for this purpose. As indicated in Chapter 4, youth transitional planning councils can serve as a key mechanism in policy formulation.

Although mayors may be more than willing to serve as youth advocates, several complicating factors need to be recognized. Beset with the variety of problems endemic to all cities, some mayors are at a loss to lend strong and direct assistance to youth at the moment.[2] Not the least of these problems are massive unemployment among urban-based adults, the absence of jobs in the inner city to which youth traditionally aspire, and an eroding tax base caused by corporate flight from urban areas. None of these problems makes the development of youth policy impossible – only more difficult.

CETA Mechanism

The CETA mechanism has demonstrated sufficient stability in enough communities across the country to serve as an important part of any youth policy. By itself, however, the CETA mechanism cannot be expected to solve the problems of youth, nor was it ever intended for this purpose. Instead, the National Commission on Youth believes that CETA must serve as one part of a comprehensive youth strategy that includes such factors as economic development plans, jobs in the private sector through training and apprenticeship programs, educational linkages, and the like.

Comprehensive Policy

The model programs reviewed in this chapter underscore one point. Successful programs cannot be defined in simplistic terms. The issue is complex, involving much more than the traditional response of jobs for youth. A broad-based response is called for, including programs that offer youth a broad range of opportunities and options. To achieve this, it is essential to develop linkages with schools, with voluntary agencies, with the private sector, and with the juvenile court system. The National Commission on Youth believes that the role of youth transitional planning councils is crucial in such collaborative efforts.

State and Federal Roles

Most local officials would welcome policy guidelines that are prescriptive but not restrictive in nature. General guidelines in terms of reducing the levels of delinquency in the community, procedures for coordinating programs and agencies, and systems analysis to improve delivery of services would allow local officials to better coordinate local policies with state and federal efforts. Finally, these guidelines must be accompanied by mechanisms to facilitate the sharing of information. This would enable local officials to see what works and then to pick and choose those aspects from successful programs that are relevant to local needs.

A Concluding Note

The overbearing observation and major lesson one learns from examining these model programs is that when given opportunities (with guidance and support) to work in responsible positions and when trusted, young people respond positively.

Where to begin? Right at home–in your own cities and communities. Creating effective, operative youth programs is no easy task. It requires taking risks. However, the challenge is only exceeded by the dangers inherent in *not* responding to youth's needs, thereby fostering the proliferation of the wave of youth crime and the resultant fear that currently permeates most major American cities. When we neglect our cities and their inhabitants, we do so at our own peril, for, in neglecting them, we imperil our society.

Notes

1. *CETA and Youth: Programs for Cities*, publication of the National League of Cities/U.S. Conference of Mayors, 1977, p. 1.

2. Remarks by Kathy Garmezy, senior staff assistant, National League of Cities/U.S. Conference of Mayors, to a meeting of the National Commission on Youth in Chicago, Ill., December 10, 1976.

9

YOUTH POLICY IN THE STATES: A SURVEY OF STATUS AND TRENDS

Recommendation 21: Development of Youth Policy at the State Level. *Each state governor should appoint a cabinet-level special assistant for youth affairs. This would enable states to coordinate more effectively existing youth policies and programs, to design policies and programs for youth where they do not presently exist, and to articulate a coherent youth policy on the state level.*

One of the tasks undertaken by the staff of the National Commission on Youth was a survey of youth policy in every state and territory of the United States. The purpose of the survey was to determine the present status of and to identify emerging trends in youth policies and programs. All of the states and territories responding to the Commission's inquiry (Appendix B) are reflected in the detailed classifications and summary analysis that follow.

The word *policy* connotes the existence of a strategy that is formulated in a cogent, deliberate, and comprehensive fashion. The term is used euphemistically in this chapter. At this time, there is precious little youth policy in the states and territories that meets this definition.

An excerpt from a letter written by the speaker of the house of representatives of a state that will go unnamed exemplifies the chronic reply to the Commission's query: "There are several major problems in the area of children and youth programs at this time in our state. . . . Among these problems are the following: the lack of coordination among the services and planning activities of the various departments of state; duplication of existing services; lack of clarity in responsibility for the provision of services; and inadequate articulation between inter-agency programs." The response is typical. A similar theme is repeated endlessly in the replies to the Commission's survey.

The responses are instructive. When reference is made to young people who attend colleges and universities, states are able to cite clearly defined higher-education policies covering these youth. When one discusses high school youth, reams of state education policy can be summoned on the spot. When one inquires, however, about the status of youth who are outside these traditional mainstream institutions, then youth policy is discussed. In short, youth policy is interpreted as applying only to young people who deviate from the traditional institutions for socialization. Recognition of this type of mind-set is important. It helps to explain why youth policy in the states is either nonexistent or lacks priority among other policy issues. Such preconceived hypotheses must be put to rest before states can develop comprehensive youth policies and programs.

On a more positive note, the Commission's survey revealed several promising programs operating on the state level. These few bright spots in an otherwise drab landscape are noted in detail in this chapter.

In recent times, state governments have tended to take their lead from the federal government, concentrating their efforts in the areas of delinquency prevention and the general control of deviancy. As a result, most youth policies and programs on the state level are circumscribed or targeted in nature. The opposite is equally true. In those states where youth policy is not targeted, it is a kind of "Open sesame!" – serving infants, children, adolescents, and young adults alike. Such efforts at general advocacy tend to be too general, too fragmented, and too irrelevant to serve the needs of such a diverse constituency.

The classifications that follow are an attempt by the National Commission on Youth to determine the present status of youth policy and programs in the states and territories and to articulate emerging trends.

Delinquency-Related Programs

The states of Alaska, Mississippi, North Dakota, Ohio, Washington, West Virginia, and Wisconsin maintain typical juvenile correctional programs. None of these programs will be treated at length in this summary.

On the other hand, Arkansas, California, Connecticut, Florida, Georgia, Louisiana, Michigan, and New York have developed delinquent youth services that go well beyond the usual custodial function, offering a variety of programs that are summarized on the following pages.

In *Arkansas*, the Division of Youth Services is moving into a service-centered concept of rehabilitation. Emphasis is placed now on placement and reintegration of youthful offenders in appropriate local environments.

The *California* Department of Youth Authority has shifted its focus from residential-based centers to community-based rehabilitation programs. A permanent staff coordinates a statewide program designed to prevent and reduce delinquency at its source – the home and the local community. Delinquency can be prevented and reduced, according to the Youth Authority, by operating programs and policies on a tripartite strategy:

1. Developing public understanding and tolerance for the diverse problems associated with the "growing up" process
2. Strengthening the attachment of young people to society through enhancement of the community's capacity to provide youth a participatory role in societal institutions
3. Reducing the number of situational inducements and opportunities for youth crime and delinquency

The Youth Authority is presently involved deeply in several subsidy and consulting programs with a dual objective in mind: to encourage home-based and community-based settings as viable alternatives to institutional incarceration.

Connecticut has phased out all but one of its correctional facilities for youthful offenders. Increased numbers of adjudicated youth, under the jurisdiction of the Department of Children and Youth Services, are diverted for placement in private residential facilities. Foster and group homes and private schools, along with residential treatment centers, form a diversified institutional mix to meet youth needs.

In *Florida,* the Division of Youth Services offers occupational guidance, counseling, and placement services for youthful offenders. The program includes job placement, a variety of counseling and guidance services, and an effort to educate the public to the rehabilitative needs of delinquent youth. The Bureau of Detention maintains a similar program to place adjudicated youth into the community in supervised settings.

Georgia, alarmed by the rate of recidivism among youthful offenders, has revamped its programs for juvenile offenders. Stress is placed on postcustodial programs. Such an approach, it is hoped, can facilitate the reentry of youthful offenders into the community. Among the community-based programs being utilized by the Division of Youth Services are individualized educational programs, personal and family counseling centers, group and recreational therapy programs, and cultural enrichment opportunities.

In *Louisiana* the Office for Youth Services functions to improve, intensify, and coordinate efforts to prevent delinquency. Three different divisions within the Youth Services Office implement these functions: Community Services screens adjudicated youth for the courts and makes recommendations for referrals to appropriate services; Field Services provides probation services and after-care; and Institutional Services administers community residential placement when commitment to the Department of Corrections is deemed unwarranted.

Michigan created the Office of Juvenile Justice Services to develop policies and procedures for a comprehensive system of juvenile treatment. To achieve this goal, the Child Care Fund, formerly used to fund foster-care programs, has been transferred from the Department of Social Services to Juvenile Justice Services. Local juvenile offender services are now funded from this revenue source.

In *New York*, all persons in need of supervision (PINS) who are referred to the Division of Youth for rehabilitative procedures are no longer automatically institutionalized. Instead, rehabilitative procedures are carried out in a variety of settings:

> Urban Homes—seven-bed units that are established in residential areas
>
> Youth Development Centers—residential and nonresidential centers especially designed to serve the needs of inner-city youth
>
> START Centers—short-term adolescent training centers built around peer-counseling programs
>
> Youth Camps—sixty-bed and forty-bed camps located in forested areas in state parks where youth split their time between forest-related labor programs and school programs
>
> Special Residential Centers—centers that serve the needs of youth who require structured group living and intensive counseling
>
> Training Schools—highly structured facilities for youth who require removal from society

Youth development and delinquency prevention are carried out by the division's Youth Bureau and Youth Service Projects. Operating on the local level, the Youth Bureau coordinates and supplements youth development efforts in both public and private sectors. Simultaneously, various Youth Service Projects attempt to detect and prevent delinquency on the local level, where it begins.

Education-Centered Programs

Several states and one territory attempt to widen the net of their youth policies and programs. Florida, Massachusetts, New Jersey, and Puerto

Rico have programs that concentrate on wider segments of youth. Typically, these programs feature an educational component, carried out through a variety of activities. Unlike the programs presented above, these operate typically under the aegis of state education departments. Generally, the programs focus on youth in the mainstream, and, as a rule, their purpose is to assist and enhance the transition of youth to adulthood through a variety of educational services and support systems.

Florida has a student services program operating in local school districts. All public school students are provided by the state with a centralized array of support services including visiting social services, psychological backup support, and occupational and placement services.

In *Massachusetts*, student service centers have been established to refer youth with special needs to appropriate state agencies. A student advisory project gives youth a forum to express their needs in direct fashion. Forty-four youth representatives sit on a council that advises the State Education Department on the needs and concerns of youth throughout the commonwealth.

New Jersey's Study Commission on Adolescent Education is engaged in developing a comprehensive educational program. The study commission has articulated the basic components of a comprehensive program and identified institutions that must play a contributing role in the program.

Puerto Rico reports a variety of programs that add new dimensions and supplement existing school programs. These include social work, transportation, medical services, and school lunch programs. Of special interest, the project Student Visits to Government Agencies is designed to interest youth in government service positions.

Youth Advocacy Programs

Youth advocacy programs are commonplace in the states and territories. They form the largest category in the Commission's survey. However, they are not monolithic in makeup. Outside of an underlying rationale to promote the interest of young people in their respective states, the agencies and programs reported below have little in common. Some are charged with enormous responsibilities, ranging from infants to young adults. Some operate only in an informal manner or an advisory capacity. A few possess political clout, but most have little or no leverage. Many agencies and programs are woefully underfunded and some are even unfunded. Some have permanent staffs, while others operate under purely voluntary arrangements.

In *American Samoa*, the Office of Youth Development cushions the transition of youth to adulthood through the pursuit of several programs.

Short-term programs emphasize citizenship education, community responsibility, and the development of youth employment opportunities. Youth are encouraged to participate in a variety of village improvement, revitalization, and recreational projects.

California's Council on Children and Youth serves as a vehicle to develop common understandings among agencies, organizations, and associations that work with children and youth on a regular basis.

Hawaii has an Office of Children and Youth that is planning to establish goals and objectives for a comprehensive policy on children and youth.

Two *Illinois* bodies operate from an advocacy position. One, the Commission on Children, studies children's needs in order to make appropriate recommendations to public and private policy planners. This commission is also charged with monitoring children's services provided by public and private agencies. The other, the Council on Youth, serves as a forum through which youth have a voice in developing policies and programs to meet their needs.

In *Indiana,* there is a Youth Council designed to coordinate planning, leadership, and service functions of public and private agencies. Much of the council's effort, however, is directed to the prevention, control, and treatment of juvenile delinquency.

Iowa has a State Youth Coordinator operating out of the Office for Planning and Programming. The coordinator administers a number of projects including all CETA-related youth programs, the Governor's Youth Opportunity Program, and the Iowa Community-Based Juvenile Corrections Program.

In *Kansas,* the Division of Services to Children and Youth operates out of the Department of Social and Rehabilitative Services. Designed to oversee the well-being of children and youth, the division is trying to develop and coordinate the numerous child and youth service programs operating within the state.

Louisiana has a Bureau of Childhood Development charged with the following duties: planning and developing more efficient delivery of children's services; recommending minimum standards for programs; and devising a councillor mechanism to provide more local input into state planning processes.

Maine has created a Children and Youth Services Planning Project to study the service needs of children and youth. The aim of the project is to streamline existing service delivery systems.

In *Massachusetts,* two agencies relate to the needs of young persons. A child advocacy agency, the Office of Children, focuses on the needs of young persons under the age of sixteen. The office plans and coordinates social services to children and maintains a regulatory and enabling presence in the areas of day-care and group-care services. The second agency, the Committee on Children and Youth, is a research and development body that makes policy recommendations to state government agencies.

The states of *Missouri, Nevada, New Hampshire,* and *New Mexico* report similar broad-based advocacy councils and commissions for children and youth. All such organizations focus on the needs of persons ranging from infants to young adults. Charged with responsibilities that are both wide and diverse, they function generally along these lines: determining priorities for children and youth; recommending policy and legislation on the basis of these priorities; providing a clearinghouse function for child and youth programs; and coordinating existing services and programs.

North Carolina operates two youth-related agencies. The Youth Council is composed of local and regional councils organized into peer groups. Organized and operated by youth, with adult supervision and guidance, local councils encourage youth to contribute to community development by means of civic-related projects. City planning agencies are encouraged to seek input from local councils when designing youth-related programs. Each local council elects representatives to regional councils, which in turn send representatives to the State Youth Advisory Council. The state council acts as a regulatory body over regional and local councils and represents youth officially in state governmental matters.

Oregon has a Governor's Commission on Youth. It is charged with wide responsibilities, including the recommendation of policy to the state legislature. Additionally, the commission serves as a clearinghouse for information pertaining to youth needs, policies, and programs.

Rhode Island's Division of Youth Development is an advocate for policy, programs, and services that strengthen and enhance the position of youth and family life in general. Some major objectives of the division include a plan to fund a newly established Intern and Volunteer Consortium, establishment of a family life–youth advocacy office, and development of a year-round service corps for unemployed youth.

In *South Carolina,* the Governor's Youth Advisory Council consists of students elected from the Governor's School for Superior and Talented Students. Periodic meetings are held with the governor for general discussions on the problems of youth.

The *Tennessee* Commission on Children and Youth carries out a diverse mandate. Charged with gathering data on the health, education, and welfare of children and youth, the commission interprets the implications of their findings to government agencies, the legislature, and to the public at large. A unique feature of the commission is its role as binding arbitrator in disputes between the Corrections Department and the courts over the status of adjudicated youth.

Texas operates two youth-related agencies. One, the Commission on Services to Children and Youth, is a research and policymaking agency. It makes policy recommendations to the state legislature and coordinates child and youth affairs among state agencies. The other, a Youth Services Division, focuses exclusively on the needs of youth. Among its diverse responsibilities are the following: training and technical assistance to local youth organizations; development of career awareness programs; assessment of specific, nonrecurrent youth problems; and development, implementation, and supervision over all statewide youth projects and programs supported from federal and state funds.

Vermont, the *Virgin Islands*, *Virginia*, and *Wyoming* have broad-based advocacy councils serving the needs of children and youth. Generally, each of the respective agencies is charged with development, implementation, coordination, and evaluation of youth policies and programs.

Miscellaneous State Programs

The survey of existing state policy and programs by the National Commission on Youth turned up several programs that have unique qualities. Colorado, New Jersey, and Utah report youth programs that are not easily classified. Because each of these programs is out of the ordinary, they deserve special mention.

Colorado's program is unique in that youth needs are serviced in part by a private agency. The Colorado Association of Child Care Institutions shares responsibilities for youth policies and programs with the Colorado Department of Social Services.

New Jersey utilizes a complex administrative structure to service a wide array of youth needs. An Office of the Public Defender within the Department of the Public Advocate supports three youth-related programs: the public defender's office is mandated to provide legal representation to indigent youth charged with criminal offenses; the Child Advocacy Program, serviced by a small specialized staff, litigates on behalf of children in the juvenile justice system; and finally, a Law Guardian Program is designed to represent the interests of children and youth who are abused and neglected.

The New Jersey Division of Human Resources is responsible for funding and coordinating programs to respond to the needs of youth, the poor, and the Spanish-speaking population. From this division, the Department of Community Affairs operates a Youth in Community Service Corps. Full-time students between the ages of fourteen and twenty-one are engaged by the corps in a number of community service projects.

The state of *Utah* has a program to meet the employment needs of youth. The Department of Employment Security operates two major projects and several smaller projects that are work-related in nature. During the summer months, Work Experience in Job Service Offices places secondary school guidance counselors in state employment offices. This experience is intended to increase the counselors' knowledge of current labor market trends, thus enabling them to better relate to their clients' job needs. A related program, Project JOIN, places computer terminals in secondary schools to enable counselors and students to keep abreast of job openings in the state labor market.

Comprehensive Youth Programs

Many states and territories responded to the National Commission on Youth's survey of existing policies and programs. Only two states, however, appear to have policies and programs that can be labeled as comprehensive in nature. Montana and Pennsylvania report policies and programs that are in place and operational. Both programs are outlined in detail.

Montana. In the opinion of the National Commission on Youth, Montana's Youth Development Bureau is the most comprehensive system operating on the state level.

Unlike most other state programs, the Montana program is not of recent vintage. The federal government provided the initial impetus for the program in 1971 through the Rural American Project. The project was established for several purposes:

To provide all of the state's youth with access to socially acceptable roles

To reduce the incidence of inappropriate and premature labeling of youth in negative roles

To reduce the amount of alienation between youth and adults

Five community workers were then placed in rural sites to develop local resources that were deemed compatible with the project's aims.

Responding to changing times and conditions since the project's inception, community workers were added, services increased, and emphasis was placed on building a systematic approach to youth programs and policies. Soon community workers were placed on a regionalized footing, serving both rural and urban areas alike on the basis of perceived needs. Eventually, as the system grew larger, the state assumed total control, establishing the Youth Development Bureau. The bureau presently operates under a diverse mandate:

> To reduce the incidence of delinquency in target areas
>
> To increase opportunities for youth to experience a meaningful adolescence, enabling them to develop into constructive adults
>
> To encourage joint needs assessment, open planning, and budget sharing and to facilitate the free flow of information between and among state agencies, along with the consumers of their services

At the present time, community workers, operating under the direction of the Youth Development Bureau, provide a wide array of services and programs to Montana youth. Here is a sample of these efforts:

> Development of a comprehensive plan for shelter, care, and detention services for juveniles pending adjudication by the courts
>
> Initiation of a continuing education program for developing effective parenting skills
>
> Development of recreational opportunities for youth during after-school hours
>
> Establishment of an intensive counseling project for recidivist probationers
>
> Utilization of high school volunteers to staff individualized and group recreational activities
>
> Assistance to school administrators to identify, strengthen, and enrich those aspects of the school curriculum that develop role access for youth, promote positive labeling of youth, and develop strong student-institutional relationships

Community workers are also assisting towns and cities across the state of Montana in various other ways: they actively assist communities to assess youth needs; they facilitate communication on youth problems by bringing together all segments of the community on issues of common interest; they develop linkages between various agencies that serve youth; they survey community resources in order to strengthen existing programs; and, finally, they design new programs and develop innovative delivery systems for youth services. The sum of these efforts is that most Montana communities have youth policies and programs that are in place and operational.

One final point needs to be mentioned. As state employees, community workers have ready access to state planning mechanisms. Such access provides important information and guidance to local agencies, which they usually lack in terms of research staffs to plan local programs. Given these back-up services, communities can provide a continuum of youth services as a part of a comprehensive state plan.

Youth policy in the state of Montana is a finely blended mixture. Local initiative and implementation are mixed deftly with firm guidelines and strong support services from the state. The National Commission on Youth applauds these efforts. It is a model that other states may usefully emulate.

Pennsylvania. Operating out of the Pennsylvania Department of Public Welfare, the Office of Children and Youth enjoys advisory capacities with all state agencies, offers direct services to young persons, and controls a number of youth-related services.

Major duties of the Office of Children and Youth include the following responsibilities:

> To assure the availability and the equitable provision of welfare services for all children and youth
>
> To consult and assist each county institution to carry out duties and functions for eligible children and youth
>
> To make and enforce all rules and regulations necessary to accomplish proper enactment of functions by county institutions
>
> To make grants to counties for services and programs
>
> To offer consultation and advice concerning the prevention of juvenile delinquency
>
> To offer consultation and advice concerning improved services and programs for juvenile delinquents

The National Commission on Youth notes one drawback to the Pennsylvania system as presently constituted: The tendency in the system at present is to focus on the needs of welfare recipients. The focus should be broadened to serve the needs of all the state's youth population.

Summary of Major Findings

The evidence assembled from the survey of youth policies in the nation's states and territories prompts the National Commission on Youth to make a number of observations in summary:

- Youth policies, programs, and practices on the state level tend to be in formative stages of development. The preponderance of evidence suggests that this is the prevailing condition rather than the exception.

- Most state youth departments and agencies do not operate as wholly independent entities. Instead, they function as parts of larger administrative units.
- Significant numbers of state youth departments function in an advisory capacity. They have neither legal mandate nor significant priority in the state administrative structure.
- Because many state youth departments are chronically underfunded or even unfunded, they do not offer significant services to other state agencies or to local communities.
- Numerous state agencies and departments are not targeted expressly to serve the needs of youth. It is commonplace for these agencies and departments to be part of a unit serving a widely diffused clientele ranging from infants to children and youth and including the family.
- A serious lack of communication and coordination among various youth-related agencies and departments is clearly evident in many states.
- There is an obvious lack of linkages between state agencies that serve youth and public and private agencies operating on local levels. Such linkages would enable states to provide much needed support services to local agencies. The end result would be a more systematic approach to the planning and development of youth policies and programs.
- Additionally, linkages between youth agencies on the state level and the private corporate sector are either insignificant or do not exist.
- Generally speaking, except for those instances noted above, states do not have comprehensive youth policies.

Evolving Youth Policy in the States

What should be the state governments' response to the problems and needs of youth? As previously indicated in this report, it is imperative that the response begin at the grassroots level. Communities should be responsible for assessing local youth needs. States, in turn, can provide funding, leadership, and important support services to assist communities in the design and implementation of youth programs. In some instances, it may be necessary for a state to mandate or administer programs and services where glaring deficiencies exist in local efforts. Finally, states must act as a fulcrum between the federal and local governments, to oversee and control funding patterns and to facilitate efficient and appropriate delivery of services.

The impressions and the understanding that emerge from the survey of youth policies and programs in the states permit the National Commission on Youth to suggest some policy recommendations. It is painfully evident to the Commission that legislation is needed at the state level to develop and maintain a comprehensive youth policy.

Where does one begin? A natural place to set this effort in motion is the place in state government where the buck stops—the governor's office. The National Commission on Youth recommends that the quest for a comprehensive youth policy be initiated by a cabinet-level appointment by each state governor of a special assistant for youth affairs.

The special assistant for youth affairs should report directly to the governor and act in a surrogate capacity in matters pertaining to youth at the state level. In this capacity, the special assistant would be empowered to represent the governor in all state-level policy and program planning sessions.

The implications of such an appointment can be enormous. Youth policy on the state level is given new impetus. Policies and programs are raised to a high level of visibility. The needs of youth are elevated to a new level of consciousness both within the echelons of state government and in the public mind on the local level. Unlike the present situation in the states, youth needs are elevated to priority status. Youth policy and programs take on new importance, leading to the articulation of a comprehensive state youth policy.

10

YOUTH POLICY
IN THE WESTERN WORLD:
LESSONS FOR AMERICA

Recommendation 22: Development of a Comprehensive National Youth Policy. *A youth policy should be developed at the federal level to serve the needs of all young persons rather than a targeted segment of the youth population. This national youth policy should be long-term in nature to allow several years start-up time in youth programs and permit the buildup of experienced personnel for effective program supervision. Implementation would include encouragement of local efforts to apply national policies in creative ways.*

We live in a global society in which the destinies of its 4 billion inhabitants are increasingly intertwined. The challenges are formidable. The problems are real and urgent. In addition to the problems of environmental ruination, resource depletion, and nuclear holocaust, the Western world is awash today in a sea of unemployed youth. Nearly 7 million young persons—a veritable nation—are without jobs.

Today's problems translate all too quickly into tomorrow's headlines. Riot, rebellion, and assassination have already reared their bloody heads among Italian youth. Youth crime is on the rise in Spain. Racism, fanned by the discontent of unemployed youth, has found its way into formerly tranquil cities in the United Kingdom.

Convinced that a macroscopic perspective might offer valuable new insights into these problems, the Charles F. Kettering Foundation in conjunction with the National Association of Secondary School Principals invited representatives from member nations of the Organization for Economic Cooperation and Development (OECD) to an unofficial conference on the international problems of youth. Conference participants from the United States, Belgium, Denmark, Ireland, the Netherlands, Switzerland, and the United Kingdom gathered in Zurich, Switzerland, in May of 1977. The Gottlieb-Duttweiler Institute provided a pleasant setting for three days of rational discourse on the problems of youth in the Western world.

The central issue around which the International Conference on Youth was organized was: Are there youth problems in the Western democracies that call for special national attention?[1]

A World Turned Upside Down

American-type economic conditions are becoming manifest in many Western nations. At Zurich, the conferees voiced concern about the alienation of youth from adult society and points of weakness in the transition to adulthood. Topping the list of concerns is youth unemployment. But that is only one aspect of a larger problem. Exacerbating the entire issue is the general softness of the world economy and uncertainty over future economic trends.

From the standpoint of youth, the situation is fraught with gloom. With their future prosperity in doubt, the impatience among Western youth is apparent. Youth are befuddled. This befuddlement generates increased hostility toward the system that produces it.

The major political worry at this point is that at some not-too-distant date, legions of unemployed youth will band together to destroy a political and economic system that offers them nothing.[2] Although this has happened to date only in Italy, the message is clear—change the system or run the risk of a return to the unrest that characterized the decade of the 1960s. Revolt, riot, and rebellion will again become the marching orders of the young.

Youth are not ready to man the barricades at this point. For the moment at least, jobs, not political uprisings, are the major concern for youth in the Western democracies.

The Key Issue of Youth Unemployment

A participant at the Zurich International Conference on Youth brought the key issue of youth unemployment into sharp focus, noting that "a few years ago, our discussions tended to be dominated by what to do about the secondary school, the university, and student unrest. Today we talk mostly about youth unemployment."

Thus has come the realization that youth unemployment is no longer a uniquely American problem. When youth unemployment first became evident on the European scene, it was dismissed quickly as a by-product of the 1973–1975 recession. But the problem has lingered on long after the recession has vanished. Now Europe is experiencing the most serious wave of youth unemployment in the postwar era. Structural unemployment is now a reality (see Chapter 5).

Some Ominous Trends

The youth unemployment rate for the twenty-four member countries in OECD currently averages 10.7 percent.[3] With but few exceptions, the problem appears to be worsening. Furthermore, the specter of joblessness is no longer confined largely to school dropouts. Secondary school and university graduates are experiencing the insidious effects of over-credentialing for the first time.

Although youth constitute only one-fifth of the OECD-nation labor force, they account for nearly two-fifths of total unemployment. The problem is most serious in Italy, Australia, and the United Kingdom; least serious in Germany, Switzerland, and Sweden. In those European nations with the most serious problems, youth unemployment rates tend to be double or triple the rates for adults. The problem is most acute in Italy, where the ratio of unemployed youth to adults is 9 to 1, in contrast to other countries where the ratio is about 3 to 1.

In Italy, discord is already evident. Overcrowded schools, overcredentialed youth, and insufficient jobs, coupled with rampant inflation, have radicalized Italian youth. Nearly half of Italy's 1.5 million unemployed youth are under twenty-five years of age; half of them are products of higher education.

The situation elsewhere, while not nearly so desperate, is not encouraging. Nearly half of the jobless in France are under the age of twenty-five; the bulk of these youth are untrained school dropouts.

Crime and political protest are on the rise in Spain. Youth are finding that most entry-level positions in the large cities and tourist centers are no longer available. Although no reliable statistics exist, estimates are that half of Spain's 900,000 jobless are under the age of thirty.

Over 40 percent of the United Kingdom's unemployed are between the ages of sixteen and twenty-five. Similar to that of France and Spain, youth unemployment is concentrated in the ranks of untrained school dropouts. In Britain, however, there is cause for additional concern. Many of the unemployed are recently immigrated black youth. If the current malaise persists, there is increased risk of racial hostility between unemployed whites and working blacks or between unemployed blacks and the white community in general.

What do the trends add up to? For the Zurich conferees, they were causes for deep concern.

Like most pressing social problems, the causes of youth unemployment on the European continent are both varied and complex. All the participants at Zurich agreed on one thing: the youth unemployment problem is widening and deepening on the European continent. The timing, the sequence, and the severity of the causes vary from country to country. Nevertheless, some explanatory factors are evident:

> Demographic trends arising from the postwar baby boom
> Competition from women whose labor force participation rate has risen sharply
> A marked slowdown in the increase of worker productivity rates
> A decline in the apprenticeship and training vacancies relative to total employment in those countries that use this method to ease the transition of youth from school to work
> Changing youth attitudes marked by a new selectivity about the types of work, the conditions of work, the hours of work, and the days of work
> Legal barriers to youth employment in regard to age, work hours, and labor conditions
> Changes in technology and the scale of industrial operations that have combined to eliminate or to reduce the number of jobs traditionally filled by young people[4]

The members of the Zurich conference were not optimistic about youth's future in the labor market, nor was a consensus attained on what is the best course of action at this moment. However, this much was clear: first, the problem is immediate, necessitating bold policy initiatives; second, flexible policies and approaches are needed, capable of being phased upward or downward in response to changes in the demographic structure, the aggregate demand for labor, and the overall rate of economic activity.

Attempts to Cope

Nearly all Western industrialized nations have responded in some form to the problem of youth unemployment. The responses vary. They include such schemes as wage subsidies, the creation of jobs for youth, and the use of traditional apprenticeship and training programs. In marked contrast to the United States, most European countries have focused their newest youth initiatives on the private sector. Chief among these is the payment of wage subsidies to employers.

Subsidizing the Cost of Labor. In addition to the traditional apprenticeship and training programs, wage subsidies have been introduced in some European nations in order to lower the cost to private employers of certain types of labor.[5] France, the United Kingdom, Sweden, and a number of other European nations have experimented with a variety of wage subsidies during the recession. A number of these schemes have been targeted exclusively for young workers entering the labor market for the first time.

One of the most ambitious schemes was introduced in France in July 1977. Significantly, the program, called Exceptional Exemption from the Employer's Social Security Contribution, is part of a package that includes a long-term strategy to reform the French secondary education system to make it more responsive to the needs of young persons entering the labor market.[6] Under the French program, private employers who hire youth twenty-five years of age and younger are exempted from paying social security taxes on the wages of those youth for a six-month period. The relief is substantial, amounting to nearly 35 percent of a beginning worker's wage. Young people who are hired must have completed their studies or occupational training within the past year. They are guaranteed employment for at least a six-month period. It should be noted that safeguards have been built into the program to prevent firms from laying off higher-paid adult workers and replacing them with subsidized youth workers.

It was precisely for this reason that the United Kingdom recently abandoned a similar program. The Youth Employment Subsidy (YES) program provided £10 per week for a six-month period to each school-leaver under the age of twenty employed in either the private sector or one of the nationalized industries.[7] At the program's peak, 45,000 youth were enrolled. By March 1978, however, the government concluded that it was paying employers a windfall subsidy and stopped the program. The chief objection was that employers tended to hire youth whom they would have hired under any circumstances, subsidy or otherwise.

Other European nations—including Ireland, the Netherlands, Italy, and all of the Scandinavian nations—have also initiated various kinds of wage subsidization programs.

The Swedish program merits especial attention because of its numerous ramifications. Swedish employers are eligible for a state subsidy of 75 percent of wage costs if, in addition to their normal recruitment efforts, they hire youth through the state employment service. Coupled with this is a specially created job program called Public Service Employment.[8] The program carries double-edged benefits in that, if a local government agency agrees to release an older, experienced worker for advanced training and hires a trainee under the age of twenty-five as a replacement, the national government pays 75 percent of the trainee's wages. At the same time, it is hoped that continued expansion in local government will enable the replacements to work their way into permanent positions after the training period is completed.

Public Service Positions. Many European countries have developed public service programs based on the rationale that governments can create jobs that can give youth valuable work experience as a prelude to permanent employment. Varied in scope, the programs range from the creation of summer community-improvement jobs to programs that encourage older workers to retire, thereby opening up positions.

European efforts in public service programs tend to be dwarfed in comparison to the public service programs mounted in the United States under the umbrella of the Comprehensive Employment and Training Act.

Among OECD member nations, only the Canada Works Program has CETA-like dimensions. Originally conceived in 1971 as the Local Initiative Program, Canada Works creates short-term (one year) employment opportunities "to counter cyclical, seasonal, and geographic employment rates." Program procedures allow established organizations and corporations to sponsor nonprofit projects for community benefit. The projects, however, cannot duplicate or compete with existing services or facilities. Despite an impressive record of achievement among Canadian youth, the Canadian government has decided to reduce the dimensions of the program by reducing its annual budget from $400 million to $250 million.

Most European programs are located in the public sector and are modest in composition. France experimented successfully with a one-year program employing 20,000 young people in priority sectors, such as postal and communication services. In Denmark, a successful job program allows municipal governments to hire young people and others at prevailing wage rates in their respective trades. Various other examples give an inkling into the scope and nature of the European effort: Finland has a program in operation that creates summer work for young persons; in France, youth are granted assistance to migrate to employment opportunities; several European nations grant full-wage subsidies to government agencies and nonprofit institutions who employ youth in positions of public service for a period of up to one year.

Apprenticeship and Job Training. Apprenticeship has been a long-established way of life in European society. This venerable institution is now being attuned to new economic realities. Germany, Austria, and Switzerland maintain traditional programs at existing levels, anticipating significant increases in the numbers of young people entering the labor market.

In other European nations, however, the continued viability of apprenticeship is under careful scrutiny; concern is raised by critics that apprenticeships exist only in those fields that are construed by youth as dead-end jobs. Openings for apprentices are declining in Germany. A marked decrease has occurred in the United Kingdom, most notably in the construction, shipbuilding, and engineering trades. Moreover, apprenticeship programs are increasingly challenged on the grounds that they offer youth poor job training, inadequate compensation, and no guarantee of a permanent position once the apprenticeship is completed.

In response to these concerns, several European countries are adjusting the apprenticeship system to changing socioeconomic conditions. Private employers are subsidized by the government during recessionary periods to take on more apprentices, to keep apprentices they would otherwise discharge, or to take on apprentices from an employer who is going out of business or, for various reasons, is unable to maintain them any longer.

There is also a tendency to treat apprenticeship as a socialization measure.[9] Some European countries now view apprenticeship as a cheap and viable alternative to advanced education. Apprenticeship is being pitched toward disadvantaged youth, including low academic achievers, along with the physically and mentally handicapped. Previously, most of this group simply left school at the end of the compulsory period and attempted to obtain unskilled work.

Current evidence suggests that as European businesses rely increasingly on American management principles and technology, employers' appetites for apprenticeship programs will wane, especially in manufacturing fields.

At this moment, most European countries are experimenting with modified mechanisms in the form of various job-training schemes, rather than expanding traditional apprenticeship programs. Nearly 200 variations were operating in Western countries in 1977.[10] The central feature of most programs is that governments simply pay a fixed stipend to private employers to train young people for specified periods. The goal of most of these programs is to impart marketable skills and provide a brief record of successful work experience to young trainees.

Despite all of these initiatives, participants at the Zurich international youth conference were not optimistic. "The steps that nations have taken," said one delegate, "are quite insufficient. Most provisions for training, for example, fail because the programs do not last long enough. Training programs last only six or eight months—then what? Then it is all over, and the youth is still out of a job."

Lessons for America

Though several European practices would be wholly unacceptable as paradigms for American programs, analysis of the various aspects of European initiatives points up some interesting perspectives. Such practices as the following would most likely be rejected in America:

> Payments to youth who have not held a full-time job since dropping out or graduating from school
> Compelling employers to hire a specified number of young people in training programs
> Encouraging early retirement in order to hire young persons as replacements[11]

On the other hand, the National Commission on Youth believes that the following practices are worth considering as possible guidelines for any comprehensive effort to reduce youth unemployment in America.

> Many programs are the products of long-term planning rather than reactions to periods of economic crisis.
> Specific program measures are an integrated part of general monetary and fiscal policy, not emergency expenditures.
> Programs are maintained on an ongoing basis, becoming operational when specified indicators point out economic deterioration.
> Programs are varied in order to meet the economic needs of a diverse population of unemployed.
> Within specific unemployment measures, youth programs carry a high priority.
> Provisions for program reduction and/or termination are developed in response to changes in the economy rather than simply for fiscal reasons.

At this point, one may ask, What are the implications for American efforts to combat youth unemployment? Several highly significant observations emerge from this comparative analysis.

• In the United States, primary emphasis is placed on creating jobs in the public sector for unemployed youth. By contrast, the locus of European efforts is in the private sector.

• Only about 25 percent of unemployed American youth under the age of twenty-one are enrolled in institutionally affiliated skill-training programs. Another 12 to 15 percent of American youth are enrolled in on-the-job training programs in private industry. The remainder of American youth are engaged in work experience programs in the public sector. In Europe, by contrast, most nations are expanding their vocational and occupational training programs on the premise that such programs are doubly cost-effective: they occupy young people and also provide valuable skill training.

• Organized labor in America has always been opposed to the subsidization of youth workers, fearing that older rank-and-file workers would be laid off in favor of cheaper labor in the form of subsidized youth. In contrast, European nations utilize wage subsidies in both the private and public sectors to encourage employers to hire and train young workers. A more palatable alternative to American labor might take the form of the payment of wage subsidies to employers who are willing to hire youth into formalized apprenticeship programs that offer comprehensive training programs in occupations where labor is in short supply. More specifically, the National Commission on Youth recommends subsidizing employers who hire youth in apprenticeship programs registered with the United States Department of Labor.

• Finally, there is a major lesson to be learned from European apprenticeship programs. While we may not have reached the upper limits of apprenticeship in America in those fields where it is still a viable alternative, it simply cannot be interjected in blanket fashion into the present labor market. The focus should be to establish a more permanent base of financial support for existing programs rather than to expand the programs into new areas.

The Transition from School to Work

For better or worse, the school is the major mechanism in Western society to assist youth in the transition to adulthood. Despite the school's limitations, industrialized nations rely heavily on it to infuse a constant supply of worker-citizens into society.

Members of the National Commission on Youth in attendance at the Zurich conference heard a familiar refrain at many of the group sessions. Delegate after delegate expressed concern over the widening gap between earning and learning. Although European countries tend to maintain more structured relationships between the school and the labor market than is the case in American society, the delegates' concern over the widening gap was apparent.

The concerns of the Zurich participants are similar to the sentiments of several other international organizations. Major studies of the transition from school to work have been undertaken by the Organization for Economic Cooperation and Development, the European Common

Market, and the Council of Europe. Three major themes have emerged from these deliberations.[12]

1. All parties agree that the preparation for work is inadequate on a number of counts. Although major criticisms are directed toward the educational system, there is unanimous agreement that the onus of blame should not rest exclusively with the schools. Rather, the entire socialization process – the family, the community, the governmental system, and employers – must share the burden of blame.

2. There is unanimous agreement that new institutions and mechanisms are needed to smooth the transition from school to work. Although schools will continue to play a major role in the transitional process, they can no longer function as exclusive entities. New institutions, some of which do not currently exist, must play a role.

3. All of the groups agree that these institutions need not, nor should they, be designed for and confined only to those youth who are unemployed; rather, they must be available to all youth.

School-Leavers

The widely proclaimed effort of getting compulsory full-time education up to age eighteen has now been largely abandoned in Europe. Particular attention is being given by OECD member nations to those youth who leave school at the minimum legal age neither earning diplomas nor taking examinations. Best present estimates are that 600,000 European youth between the ages of sixteen and eighteen leave school annually to seek work. This amounts to a pool of approximately 2.4 million youth seeking unskilled entry-level jobs. Only recently, the International Labour Office reports that a number of European governments have issued shrill warnings to school-leavers that a deteriorating labor market awaits them.[13]

Efforts to meet the needs of school-leavers vary from country to country, dependent on the structure of the educational system and the training opportunities available to those who drop out. French and Swedish programs were often cited at the Zurich conference. *France* has embarked on a plan for youth, aged fourteen to sixteen, who are experiencing trouble in conventional school programs. A legal escape clause in the new French educational law permits fourteen-year-olds to enter preapprentice and prevocational training. The school system is negotiating with employers to establish permanent programs to hire early school-leavers under these arrangements. *Sweden*, where 30 percent of the students drop out of the upper secondary school system, has introduced a host of measures to give students a second chance. Short academic and vocational courses, lasting two or three months, have been introduced. A work experience component has been added to the program. The credit system has been arranged so that one can participate in these flexible programs and not suffer a delay in graduation dates.

Work Experience Programs

Members of the National Commission on Youth note a general reluctance among European educators to develop work experience programs in the schools in lieu of the traditional apprenticeship and training programs. One exception to this norm is the Swedish educational system.

Work-oriented comprehensive schools are already well established throughout Sweden as a result of long-range planning efforts. Career education and vocational education are infused throughout the compulsory phase of schooling, which ends at age sixteen. All youth, male and female alike, between the ages of fifteen and sixteen are required to spend three weeks in a work experience program in some phase of the industry. In the upper secondary school, which most students attend to the age of eighteen, students are required to complete a vocational *pratique* of several months' duration.

Coupled with the school curriculum is a recently introduced Outreach Program that gives students occupational information, counseling, and job placement services. The service operates along the following lines: committees are formed in every Swedish community consisting of school representatives, the employment service, and a host of community agencies. Each committee monitors the progress of all youth who leave school at age sixteen, following them until the age of twenty. Guidance counselors perform similar services for youth who remain in school through the upper secondary phase.

The delegates who came to Zurich sought, among other things, to articulate the thrust of European efforts to improve the transition from school to work. In this vein, the following consensus was attained.

> There is movement in many nations to reinforce career information, guidance, and job placement services.
> Increased cooperative action is apparent among a number of diverse parties and institutions – schools, employers, government agencies, and voluntary organizations – who are involved in the transitional process.
> Work experience programs are starting to develop in reaction to the isolating effects of the educational process.
> Community participation is mentioned increasingly, particularly in terms of sending both teachers and students into the world of work to gain firsthand experience about various kinds of occupations.

Planning for the Longer Run: National Policy

European countries, on the whole, tend to regard the transition from school to adulthood as a serious social problem. This concern is heightened by the realization that no longer will they be able to absorb with relative ease each group of new entrants into the labor market. Without giving the needs of youth precedence over those of adults, Europe is concerned particularly about three aspects of youth unemployment.[14]

1. Difficulty in obtaining a first job is seen as especially damaging to the individual. The result is an overriding concern for the needs of all unemployed youth. Programs are designed to meet individual needs rather than the needs of specific disadvantaged groups.

2. The movement of young people into the labor force is regarded as the key mechanism in maintaining, developing, and renewing the ranks of labor. If cyclical or extraordinary events reduce or alter the intake of new entrants, the economy and the nation stand to lose. In short, the national interest is at stake.

3. A significant rise in youth unemployment is feared because of its attendant political and social consequences: rioting, terrorism, and increases in crime, delinquency, and other costly outlets.

It is interesting to note, by comparison, that youth policy in the United States gives slight note to the first two aspects and tends to concentrate on the final aspect. Furthermore, this concentration is focused largely on unemployed youth in major urban centers.

Without discounting the significance of inner-city youth, it is fair to say that the overall effort for needy unemployed American youth—the vast majority of whom are white—has been inadequate. And herein lies an important point: the concern for the individual as part of a comprehensive youth policy is notably absent in the United States. The clear lesson is that all youth without jobs are potential problems and may cause damage to the social fabric of the nation. Therefore, the National Commission on Youth recommends that comprehensive youth policies and programs be designed to serve the needs of all youth on an individualized basis.

Perhaps the major point of difference between European and American policy approaches is that Europeans, while allowing for local flexibility, deal at the national level with policymaking and program implementation. Particularly noteworthy is the European tendency to include several years of lead time or start-up time in the programs. Such features yield long-range dividends in the development of an experienced cadre of intermediate-level supervisors ready to perform key tasks as programs are fully implemented.

Many European countries ascribe cabinet-level importance to youth affairs. Some ministries are oriented toward sports and culture, others toward education, and still others toward jobs or vocational training. Although not necessarily comprehensive in scope, all serve to give youth policy a sense of mission, direction, articulation, and much-needed visibility.

In France, for example, there is a Ministry of Youth and Sport, which concentrates on the leisure interests of youth. West Germany has a Ministry of Youth, Family Life, and Health, which oversees various aspects of youth policy including education, apprenticeship, work, leisure, family relations, and health.

The United Kingdom takes a slightly different tack. The National Youth Bureau, a private agency, is funded by various government agencies. Operating with umbrella responsibilities, it serves as a resource, training, and policymaking center for British youth workers. Much of the bureau's effort is devoted to evaluating models of good practices and making policy recommendations to appropriate government departments.

The Swedish approach to policy formulation is particularly illuminating. Secure in a rich tradition of youth programs, Swedish policy has evolved to a point where it is seldom necessary to legislate new programs at crisis intervals. Each year the Labor Market Board submits a general budget request with general headings but without specific allocations. In addition to this flexibility, if deemed necessary, the board is authorized to overspend its general budget allocation.

The aim of these various Swedish policy initiatives is clear. The intent is to address fundamental issues and formulate comprehensive policies rather than to operate from patchwork or catch-up approaches. The focus is on the development of excellence, not survival in an atmosphere of crisis. The close resemblance between announced policy and actual programs, the sophisticated infrastructure by which programs are transferred to local levels, the tempering of national policy to local conditions, and the cooperative efforts between governmental departments—all testify to a national commitment to youth and stand in glaring contrast to current American policies and practices.

A Final Note of Caution

Comparative analysis is always a risky enterprise. In this spirit, the National Commission on Youth interjects a cautionary note. Understandably, the temptation is great to conclude that America should emulate European successes as expeditiously as possible. But any rush to judgment must be avoided. Oftentimes, as Eric Sevareid warns, the chief cause of problems lies in the nature of the proposed solutions.

No one denies that many of the problems that bedevil American youth are similar to problems confronting youth in other industrialized nations. But the atmosphere and circumstances in which problems arise and to which solutions are proposed is crucial. More specifically, it is exceedingly difficult, if not impossible, to isolate the effects of policies and programs from underlying economic and social differences. For example, there is a necessary trade-off to be made between upward mobility and individual freedom on one hand and high unemployment rates on the other. American youth experience higher unemployment than many of their European counterparts, but they also tend to be employed at fewer dead-end jobs. European youth tend to fit into job patterns without the frictional aspects generated by extended periods of search and experimentation in entry-level jobs. To date, no system has been devised whereby young people could be employed on a continuing basis while simultaneously pursuing career options to upgrade themselves.[15]

The point is simple. It would be idealistic, simplistic, and downright irresponsible to say that all that is necessary to solve youth unemployment and to smooth the transition of youth to adulthood is to see how others do it and then to emulate their successes.

This realization, perhaps, was among the most valuable insights derived from the International Conference on Youth. It is apparent to the National Commission on Youth that European countries have learned valuable lessons from the pioneering efforts of American reformers. In such areas as programs for minority youth, second-chance educational opportunities, and work experience programs, Europe has little to teach America. On a different note, it is apparent that America has much to learn from the European approach to policy formulation at the national level. What is most apparent is that we can learn from each other. And this was precisely the reason why the Zurich conference was convened.

Notes

1. A report on the conference has been published by the National Association of Secondary School Principals. See *Youth to Adulthood: Impasse and Dilemma in the Western World*, National Association of Secondary School Principals, Reston, Va., 1978.

2. "Pursuing Jobs, Not Politics," *The Economist*, December 3, 1977.

3. Organization for Economic Cooperation and Development, *High Level Conference on Youth Unemployment: Diagnosis* (item 4), Paris, France, November 9, 1977, p. 3.

4. Beatrice Reubens, *Youth Unemployment,* Hearing before the Joint Economic Committee, Congress of the United States, Ninety-Fourth Congress, September 9, 1976, Washington, D.C. (U.S. Government Printing Office, 1976), p. 43. Also see OECD, *High Level Conference on Youth Unemployment: Diagnosis,* pp. 13-16.

5. Remarks of William Hewitt, administrator, Office of Policy, Evaluation, and Research, Employment and Training Administration, Department of Labor, at a meeting of the National Commission on Youth in Washington, D.C., April 28, 1978.

6. For a comprehensive analysis of the French program, see Organization for Economic Cooperation and Development, *High Level Conference on Youth Unemployment: Inventory of Measures Concerning the Employment and Unemployment of Young People* (item 5), Paris, France, November 23, 1977, pp. 56-58.

7. Ibid., p. 65.

8. Remarks of Dr. Beatrice Reubens, professor of economics, Columbia University, New York, at a meeting of the National Commission on Youth, Miami, Fla., February 8, 1977.

9. Ibid.

10. A complete listing is contained in OECD, *High Level Conference on Youth Unemployment: Inventory of Measures Concerning the Employment and Unemployment of Young People* (item 5), Paris, France, November 23, 1977, 210 pp.

11. Reubens, *Youth Unemployment,* p. 44; and remarks of William Hewitt to National Commission on Youth.

12. Remarks of Dr. Beatrice Reubens to National Commission on Youth.

13. *Youth Unemployment in Industrialized Market Economy Countries,* International Labour Office, Geneva, Switzerland, April 1978, pp. 61-73.

14. Remarks of Dr. Beatrice Reubens to National Commission on Youth.

15. James Coleman, *The Teenage Unemployment Problem: What Are the Options?* report of Congressional Budget Office Conference, October 14, 1976 (U. S. Government Printing Office, Washington, D.C., 1976), p. 48.

PART 4

EVOLVING YOUTH POLICY

11

NEW ENVIRONMENTS FOR YOUTH

Recommendation 23: Transition Schools. *Transition schools should be established for the final years of secondary education. These would offer high school students a wide variety of options to enable them to move beyond the classroom into the neighborhood and the community to complete their education.* Transition schools, operated by the public school system, *would afford youth opportunities to pursue special interests, to explore career options, to learn new skills, and to test newly acquired competencies in internships and apprenticeships in a community-based environment.*

Recommendation 24: Optional Learning Centers. *Optional learning centers should be established to serve as safety nets for youth who find transition schools inappropriate for their educational needs.* Operating independently of the public school system, *optional learning centers would provide jobs, service opportunities, and vocational apprenticeships in the community. Youth transitional planning councils would be responsible for the placement of students in jobs and for monitoring their progress in field-work settings.*

Recommendation 25: Vocational Education in a Community-Based Environment. *Vocational education should be shifted from the high schools into the community, where it more properly belongs. The concept of performance contracting should be revived to monitor the learning of apprentice and vocational skills that are taught by community-based institutions.*

The final two chapters of this report represent a beginning rather than an ending. They reflect a vision of youth not as they are, but as they may become. Prescriptive and descriptive in nature, Chapters 11 and 12 represent a holistic approach to the transition of youth to adulthood. They embrace the key institutions involved—the home, the school, the community, and, finally, the government.

Admittedly, many young people develop passably well in the existing transitional environment. In recent times, however, serious erosion has taken place in the home, the school, and the community. A consequence of this erosion is that increased numbers of youth need assistance as they move toward adulthood.

If the future of the nation is in the hands and minds of youth, then new environments must be designed that will enable youth to attain their full potential. The purpose of this chapter is to suggest more appropriate environments for youth.

The Erosion of the Transitional Environment

The problems that bedevil youth today are the problems of success. They are essentially problems resulting from our fabulous successes in technology, in industrial management, and in raising educational (and expectational) levels. So insulated have we become as a society, says Elise Boulding, "that we feel neither heat nor cold, wind nor rain, love nor hate, and never know what phase the moon is in unless we look at the calendar."[1]

To understand these problems, it is necessary to look more closely at the long-term trends that have caused them. Robert Heilbroner calls this the "great ascent" – the long trend of modernization and economic development that contains within it such dynamic underlying stages as the growth of empirical science and the industrial revolution. In preindustrial society most people were involved in work within the home to meet their own needs and those of a limited community. The money economy was not central – most exchanges occurred outside the money economy. Behavior fell largely into traditional roles.

As American society has become industrialized, specialized, secularized, and urbanized during the "great ascent," youth have increasingly become more isolated from society. All the problems typically listed as the "problems of youth" in the transition to adulthood derive, to an important extent, from this fundamental systematic trend.

Societal response to these problems has been disappointing at best. The present institutional environment severely constricts young people because it tends to be dominated by one activity – sitting in a classroom isolated from the real world of work and adult society. In sharp contrast to this state of affairs, one is reminded of the centuries old admonition of Seneca: "As long as you live, keep learning how to live."

But herein lies a problem. There are few direct opportunities available to young people to contribute to the maintenance of the family and even fewer opportunities for them to help with their parents' occupations. Exacerbating this isolationism, as previous chapters have pointed out, are such measures as minimum-wage laws, compulsory schooling regulations, and laws regulating the conditions of child labor.

The net result of this isolation is that young people proceed to adulthood in lock-step fashion, consigned to "drying out on [their] own little twigs, never nourished by the freshness of different perceptions of folk in other age groups, on other parts of the vine, never experiencing that we are all branches of the one vine."[2]

This age segregation gives rise to a number of troubling implications. As Commissioner Urie Bronfenbrenner points out, it leaves the family, already in a weakened state, as almost the sole institution to foster and to facilitate cross-age communication.

Age segregation also fosters alienation among the young. Rebuffed in their attempts to be integrated into adult society, youth feel uninterested and hostile toward their environment. One need not look far for the consequences of this alienation. They are reflected in the rise in the rates of crime, delinquency, violence, and vandalism in the schools and on the streets and, sadly, are also reflected in the frightening runaway and suicide rates among the young.

It is one thing to detail the erosion of the existing environment—the breakdown of the family, the omissions of the school, and the deterioration of the community. It is something else to identify new sources of leverage for these traditional institutions of socialization and, when found, to mobilize such leverage to create new environments for youth. To this task, the Commission turns.

New Environments for Youth

The proposals of the National Commission on Youth are tempered by yesterday's failures, encompass today's successful policies and practices, and respond to tomorrow's challenges. Future needs call for a shorter, more carefully planned transitional period that involves all youth in a variety of community-based activities in which they take on increasing initiative and responsibility.

A necessary first step in the design of new environments for youth is to break down the age segregation barriers that presently isolate youth from society. The removal of these barriers raises a host of fundamental questions and embraces a whole range of options. For example, how much protection is necessary for youth to make the transition to adulthood in optimum fashion? How specialized should a young person's activities be during various stages of the transitional process?

Answers must also be found for questions pertaining to the role of the major institutions that figure into the transitional process. Such broadly based questions include the following: What degree of independence should young persons have from the home, the school, and from employers during the transitional process? What should be the division of authority between the home, the school, and the community over the young person during various stages of the transition? Who is taking ultimate responsibility with regard to young persons in the environments in which they develop into adults?

It is probably unrealistic to expect conclusive answers to queries so broadly based. Nevertheless, the Commission believes that these questions, along with a host of others, must be raised on a continuing basis in order to build new environments for the transition of youth to adulthood.

What needs to be done? The National Commission on Youth recommends that concerted efforts be made to break down the formidable barriers that presently separate the institutions of socialization from each other. The interconnections, not the isolation of institutions from each other, need to be reemphasized. Society must rediscover what was known in a much earlier period of Western civilization – that we get competent human beings when we support the institutions that make for competent human beings. The ancient Greeks realized this. The secret of the *Paidea* was that the business of education was the business of the entire society.

The new question to be asked, then, is not how much schooling should youth have, but what are the most appropriate environments in which youth can make the transition into adulthood?

A more appropriate environment for the transition of youth to adulthood must certainly emphasize schooling but must not be limited exclusively to the school. It must include the home and the community. Strong connecting bonds must be forged between each of these entities. In such newly designed environments, youth are not limited to the passive role of students but are cast in a variety of different roles: roles involving care of the young and the old alike; roles involving maintenance and repair of the environment; roles involving interdependent work with others toward a goal outside of one's self; and, finally, roles involving direct interaction with adults in a productive society.

The Home Environment

The family is the cornerstone of our society. It is our premier national resource, the single most essential institution for our society to survive and to function properly. Ultimately, the strength of our nation is directly related to the strength of the family unit. There is an old Chinese proverb that states, "Nobody's family can hang out a sign, 'Nothing matters here.'" The relationships that the family engenders are what Urie Bronfenbrenner calls "the juice of life," encompassing the entire spectrum of human behavior – the sorrows and the joys, the longings and the achievements, along with the frustrations and the intense loyalties that make up the drama of human life.

The family, more than any other single institution, reflects the societal changes that characterize life in America. Even to the most callous observer, it is now apparent that a kind of ecology exists in Western modern industrialized society that is inimical to the needs of young people.[3]

In early American society, most families lived a subsistence-type existence, maintaining themselves on farms or from family-controlled shops. Parents and children labored side by side in such cooperative ventures. In these circumstances, each young person knew exactly what his place was in the order of things, what his reponsibilities were, and what contributions he made to the maintenance of the family.[4]

Modern youth, by comparison, can no longer experience similar feelings of personal security and the satisfaction that comes from the pursuit of excellence. Significant ways in which the family aided youth in the transition to adulthood have diminished: fewer tasks are assigned to youth that contribute to the maintenance of the family; fewer opportunities exist for youth to participate in joint occupational enterprises with their parents; and fewer situations allow young persons to assume adult responsibilities or to try out adult roles.[5]

Man is a social animal. Above all other species, survival requires that the young learn from the old. The capacity for human achievement beyond human imagination lies precisely in the ability of adults to pass on knowledge and skills to the young. From this nurturing process, mutual benefits develop along the following lines: "The old, with their wisdom and earthbound experience, are necessary correctives to the soaring fantasy, untested idealism, and despair of youth. But the intensity, idealism, and despair of youth are equally needed correctives to the pragmatism, cynicism, and pallor of age. It is important, desperately important, that we accept youth for their idealism and that they accept us for our experience."[6]

Learning to be a responsible citizen and to bear the consequences of one's actions demands a wide variety of learning experiences coupled with a gradual increase in responsibility. The problem is that the home cannot provide the diversity of experience that most youth need to develop this sense of confidence. This is where support systems, particularly the school and the community, must play a crucial role.[7]

Contrary to popular belief, the family is not destroying itself. What is destroying the family is the indifference of the rest of society. New environments must be created to enable families to do what they do better than anyone else. Young people and adults need to be able to enter each other's worlds.

The need to develop a variety of family support systems in the school and in the community is acute. To this need the National Commission on Youth gives its attention.

The School Environment

Consider the realities of the present system of schooling. We have created an educational environment in which youth associate only with other youth. Under the present system it is possible—in fact, quite probable—that, when young people graduate from high school, they have never been in a situation in which someone was dependent upon them. Oftentimes this situation is prolonged for another four, six, or even eight years when young persons attend college or go on to professional schools.

Curiously, the system produces many youth who are filled with humanistic values but who are totally deficient in humanistic skills. It is entirely possible to graduate from high school, college, or professional school, never having held a baby, never having had the opportunity to care for a child or an elderly person, never having had to be with someone who was lonely, disconsolate, sick, or dying.

What a terrible deprivation this is—to be sixteen, or eighteen, or twenty-two years old and not to know how to care for or cope with a fellow human being who isn't young, statuesque, and well dressed.

The Commission believes that the most important thing that schools can do for young people is to introduce a "curriculum for caring." The hallmark of this approach is that students don't engage in learning about people who care, but that they participate in care. They learn about caring in those institutions in the community—in business and industry, in government, in service agencies, and in voluntary organizations – where adult behavior is the model, where responsibility is assumed, and where real consequences flow from one's actions.

Models for a New Educational Environment

If an appropriate new environment is to be designed, it must be done on the basis that *schooling is not all of education.* Once this assumption is recognized, it is possible to design a wholly new educational environment, an environment that is more compatible with the community than is the traditional school setting. Recognizing that a certain strength is derived from a diversified approach to any task, the National Commission on Youth recommends the following models for a new educational environment.

The Transition School

As students progress toward the final years of formal education, high schools should offer a variety of options that enable youth to move into the community beyond the classroom. Students should be able to pursue their special interests, to explore career options, and to test their skills and competencies in internships or apprenticeships.

Alternatives might be offered to include:

- A *high school arts center*, linked to community theater groups, galleries, museums, and orchestras, that could provide talented students with apprenticeships and internships
- A *school-business partnership*, in which local business and industry would provide on-the-job training and apprenticeships for students one or two days a week and would enable students to hone existing skills, acquire new competencies, and gain some work experience
- A *health-professions school*, which would be linked to hospitals and clinics in the community providing both service and occupational opportunities for young people while they are still in school
- A *social-service school*, with ties to community institutions, that could offer apprenticeships so that young people could gain service experience in retirement homes and hospitals and in city parks and senior-citizen centers (As mentioned in Chapter 3, if National Youth Service becomes a reality, students would be able to earn credit toward graduation or for educational entitlements through various forms of service to their community and to the nation.)

- A *university in the school* concept that could offer advanced academic courses to academically talented youth in mathematics, the sciences, or the humanities

The result of the transition school[8] would be to transform the high school into a community-based school. Operating under the aegis of the high school, students would be placed in learning sites in the neighborhood, and community groups could come into the school to use the facilities and to offer their support.

The Optional Learning Center

Some young people would find the environment of the transition school too restrictive for their educational needs. The optional learning center would serve as a safety net for potential dropouts. Unlike the transition school, it would operate independently of the public school system. Significant alternatives would be available in the optional learning center in the form of job, service, and vocational apprenticeships and internships.

Through a free and easy process, high school students at the age of fourteen would be able to enroll in a community-based learning environment. Public funds in the form of per-pupil expenditures would transfer with them to participating organizations, businesses, and agencies. These community-based enterprises would provide action-learning programs for their self-selected student body.

The optional learning center would place students in wide-ranging alternatives, following a careful evaluation of students' interests and capacities. Once appropriate placements are made, students' education would alternate between small-group seminars and work in the field.

The optional learning center would operate under the jurisdiction of the youth transitional planning council (Chapter 4), the function of which would be to assure the successful placement and progress of students in field-work situations. The variety of educational alternatives for students should be limited only by the needs of participating youth and the imagination of the council. The goal is to manage the system so that young persons are provided with educational environments that are compatible with their needs.

National Youth Service

As noted in Chapter 3, service-learning on either a full-time or a part-time basis would be a viable alternative for some high school students. Through service to the community or to the nation, students could earn academic credit toward a high school diploma. At the same time, students would be learning marketable job skills and earning entitlements for education beyond high school.

Implementing a New Educational Environment

The achievement of a new educational environment for the transition of youth to adulthood necessitates new policies and practices to encourage, aid, and support this reconstructive effort. To facilitate this process, several procedures seem imperative.

The Considered Alternative

The rejection of school by large numbers of youth calls into question traditional notions that all young people should remain within the conventional school framework until the age of sixteen. There is nothing sacrosanct about this age. If anything, it should merely mark the end of one phase of the educational process and the beginning of another.

It is precisely at the point of the legal school-leaving age, the traditional dropout period in American education, that constructive educational alternatives must be made available to youth. In this spirit, the National Commission on Youth proposes the concept of the considered alternative.

The choice of words is deliberate. It implies not an end to the educational process but, rather, the choice of a more appropriate environment. The Commission rejects such pejorative terms or labels as *dropping out, stopping out, furlough,* or *break.* Such terms imply that youth simply turn off their brains and vegetate during these periods. But most young people who opt for this alternative do not abandon education, only schooling in a formal sense. Instead of dropping out, they move into an educational environment of a different kind, one more community-oriented than school-oriented.

The concept of the considered alternative holds out the possibility that young people will be able to make infinitely better choices about their educational directions when and if they decide to return to a more conventional educational environment.

Opportunity Vouchers

Some form of educational entitlements must receive serious consideration in any plan for designing new educational environments for youth.

As proposed in Chapter 3, the National Commission on Youth

recommends that youth receive educational entitlements in exchange for service rendered to the community and to the nation.

A point to stress is that these vouchers would not be utilized in an identical manner. Ultimately, each individual will decide how to use the vouchers, if at all. When utilized, the vouchers should pay for any type of educational experience that one chooses, at any point in life. Thus, individuals might utilize them to attend law school, to learn the trade of airline mechanic, or to become a barber, truck driver, or teacher.

There is simply no logical reason to divide life into a series of time traps—youth for education only, adulthood for work, and old age for nothing. If this entrapment is to be ended, learning must be viewed as a lifelong enterprise.

The logic of the National Commission on Youth in proposing what it calls the opportunity vouchers is based on the proposition that the process of learning does not stop at the high school or college level. It is a lifelong proposition. Furthermore, at a time when the student population is decreasing rapidly, causing colleges and other institutions of learning to compete for students in ways that raise serious concerns, some form of educational entitlement appears infinitely sensible.

Teacher Internships

Young people acquire most of their knowledge about the world of work from their teachers. But teachers know mostly about teaching and schools. Accordingly, the National Commission on Youth believes it imperative that teachers have increased opportunity for internships in the world of work. Acquisition of such firsthand experience should make teachers infinitely more effective in teaching and in counseling young people about career options in the world of work.

Flexible Scheduling

Schools will have to establish flexible schedules if community-based education is to operate in optimum fashion. Some secondary school students will work part-time while attending school on a regular basis; other students will be engaged in full-time jobs and attend school on a part-time basis. This will necessitate scheduling increased numbers of classes in the late afternoon or in the evening. Arrangements must also be made to allow students to work in the community for a semester or more, then to return to their studies on a full-time or part-time basis.

The Commission recommends that secondary schools begin experimenting with flexible scheduling arrangements as increased numbers of young people seek out alternatives to the conventional school environment. Schools might consider experimenting with a four-day or four-and-one-half-day week. Under this plan, in the released time students would be engaged in a variety of community-based experiences while teachers would be monitoring these experiences or be engaged in in-service learning activities.

Revisiting Some Traditional School Functions

It is apparent to the Commission that schools can no longer assume the *whole* task of educating youth. The time has come for the secondary school to shift some of these responsibilities to the community, where they more properly belong. In so doing, secondary schools might be free to concentrate on doing better that which they still do better than any other societal institution: assisting the cognitive development of young people through the correlation and expansion of factual knowledge and helping them to sharpen their intellectual skills.[9] Historically, public schools have also been a great equalizing force in American society. Both these functions must be renewed with increased commitment.

Schools as Scholarly Communities

The National Commission on Youth wishes to emphasize that the new environments they envision do not in any manner denigrate the need of youth for a sound basic education. Schools must reaffirm with increased vigor the primacy of basic education in terms of verbal and mathematical skills. If young people continue to be graduated from high school who cannot read, write, and enumerate, the school system has failed.

Schools as Just Communities

The tragic events of the People's Temple in Guyana have sensitized the nation to the fact that our secularized society has created a dangerous spiritual/moral vacuum in the lives of young people.[10] Religious institutions, like other supportive institutions such as the schools, have been called into question and their importance diminished.

Yet, young people continue to respond to innate spiritual/moral instincts. The result is a gap in young people's development that increasingly is being filled by irrational and bizarre cultish forms.

The Commission believes that the secondary school must continue to provide an environment in which youth can experience directly the meaning of justice and democracy. Schools must continue to be places where the ideals of justice and fair play predominate.

The "care of the soul" is as difficult a task today as it was in the time of Socrates. Perhaps more than at any other time in history schools must play a vital role in filling the moral void in the lives of young people.

The Community Environment

In one of the deliberative sessions of the National Commission on Youth, Commissioner Urie Bronfenbrenner said something that was noted carefully by other members of the Commission. In a simple, but profound observation on a lifetime of scholarship, he said,

> If there is anything that comes out of my work on the family, it is that parents are only the first and, perhaps, not even the most important people in the child's life. Above all else, it is very critical that young people know other adults. We live in an age-graded society. It is necessary to build bridges between the schools and the world of work so you don't get this crazy situation which you have now where you don't get to know what work is until you graduate from high school. You don't get to know your own parents as workers. You don't get to know what workers are like as human beings.

If the vision of a new environment for the transition of youth to adulthood is to become a reality, it rests on the recognition that the community must serve as a major learning resource. It involves nothing less than breaking down the barriers that have existed for so long between learning and earning. For schools, it means opening doors that have long remained closed to the community. For business and industry, it means taking on a new function—teaching job skills and competencies to young people. Finally, if youth are to become responsible and productive adults, such reality means interacting with a variety of adults in different community institutions and actually participating in work tasks.

The magnitude of this change raises many questions: Who will pay the costs of community-based education? What educational tasks can the community perform more effectively than the schools? What types of controls need to be established to monitor the effectiveness of community-based instruction? Can educators and industrialists operate as equal partners in joint learning ventures? Answers to these and other questions must be thrashed out before the community can serve as a major learning resource.

The Issue of Funding

If learning is to become a product of the workplace, private enter-prise must be paid from the public purse much as public schools are. The realities of the marketplace dictate that the private sector cannot be expected to play the role of beneficent godfather. This is not an in-surmountable barrier. As pointed out in Chapter 5, a variety of incen-tives – grants, tax rebates, and perhaps even limited wage sub-sidies – might be offered to businesses that establish programs that provide youth with work opportunities.

Perhaps in times past society has been too willing to accept the government as the provider of first resort rather than of last resort. The Commission believes that the effects of this assumption on work opportunities for youth need attention. As long as this rationale goes unchallenged, the expansion of jobs in the public sector will be offset by the shrinkage of job opportunities in the private sector. At some point it becomes self-defeating. As job opportunities disappear in the private sector, the rationale and the demand for government-created jobs increase. Ultimately, the point is reached when sizable numbers of young people will work for the government. "It is hard to imagine," observes Commissioner Gordon Bowden, "that this would be an im-provement for youth or for the rest of us."

Vocational Education

The strengthening of vocational education is crucially important in any design for new environments for youth. The National Commis-sion on Youth believes that secondary schools have failed in the area of vocational education. No single issue before the Commission pro-duced greater agreement. Vocational education as it is presently taught in most high schools is an expensive failure.

The Youth Employment Demonstration Projects Act (YEDPA), passed by Congress in 1977, required that a minimum of 22 percent of the funds be spent on school programs. It is estimated that as much as 55 percent of this money from the Department of Labor has ended up in school programs, much of it in existing vocational education pro-grams. The Commission notes that more than $350 million has been funneled into vocational education during FY 1978.[11]

Much of the present debate over the status of vocational education clearly misses the mark.[12] The issue is not whether young people need vocational education or traditional academic education. They need both. John Gardner states it this way: "An excellent plumber is in-finitely more admirable than an incompetent philosopher. The society which scorns excellence in plumbing because it is a humble activity and tolerates shoddiness in philosophy because it is an exalted activity will have neither good plumbing nor good philosophy. Neither its pipes nor its theories will hold water."

The argument against the effectiveness of vocational education in the high schools is the mounting evidence that the schools have been too little concerned with the application of what is taught, especially its relevance to work.

- Expensive equipment, materials, and space needed to create effective school programs are rendered obsolete over a comparatively short span by technological advances and changes in local and national job markets.
- Only a limited number of facilities can be constructed due to the enormous start-up costs associated with vocational programs. The result of this is that youth are forced to opt for vocational education at an early age in order to secure placement in the program.
- Premature job entry greatly lessens future career options for youth.
- Young people are being trained in skills for which the demand is declining or for jobs that no longer exist.

For these reasons, then, the National Commission on Youth recommends that vocational education be shifted from the schools into a community environment where it more properly belongs.

As vocational instruction comes under the auspices of community-based institutions, performance contracting should be revived to monitor the learning of vocational skills. The Commission believes that the concept of performance contracting is an eminently sensible practice whose past failures can be easily explained. They lie not in the nature of the concept but in its placement in the school instead of the community.

The contractual relationship should operate along the following lines: Educators and employers should mutually specify the competencies to be learned. Employers would be paid on both a per capita and a pro rata basis. If the specified minimum competencies were not achieved by student trainees, no payment would be made; if there were a greater than anticipated increase in student achievement, a bonus would be paid to the participating employer.

In essence, then, the contracting firm's profit would be tied directly to the level of student achievement in job-related competencies. In this community-based environment, performance contracting is an idea that has come of age.

Monitoring Community-Based Education

The mention of performance contracting raises the related issue of the role of the school in monitoring community-based learning experiences. A community-based curriculum implies new roles not only for students but also for administrators and teachers. Significant numbers of school personnel must be relocated into the community to develop effective linkages between the school and community-based institutions and to monitor and evaluate the quality of learning experiences in these institutions.

The Commission emphasizes that learning does not occur simply by being on the job. The process of learning, like life itself, has no "free lunches." If community-based learning is to become a widely accepted educational alternative, it will be necessary to establish carefully the performance standards and the related benefits that will be expected to accrue from these experiences. Some of these competencies can be based on demonstrated behaviors and productive performance tests; others can be based on performance ratings of supervisory personnel; still other evaluative criteria will depend on the inventiveness, the imagination, and the resourcefulness of the supervisory cadre. The point is that demonstrated skills, competencies, and credentials must become a carefully documented part of the education-work record of participants.[13]

This will not be an easy task. Learning in the community—in the "school of hard knocks"—is a spontaneous process, often difficult to measure. It is a type of incremental learning that slowly builds up as one participates in the arena of life.

More than likely, community environments will not affect the learning and development of young persons in similar ways. It is entirely probable that similar environmental antecedents will produce differing consequences depending on the match-up or mix of those variables that define human individualism.[14] For example, two short-term consequences that may be potentially disruptive to youth merit special attention. For some youth, prolonged separation from their peer group may engender feelings of loneliness, insecurity, hostility, and even alienation toward the community learning environment, and similar feelings may also be generated among youth who are unable to cope with the ordinary stresses—the "hard knocks" that arise from being on the job.[15]

Answers to these questions and others can only be worked out over time and will vary according to the particular community, the particular learning environment, and the particular individuals involved. Nearly a century ago, Herbert Spencer cautioned against planning because, whatever planners try to do, things usually turn out differently.

The National Commission on Youth does not expect instant success from these proposals to develop new environments for the transition of youth to adulthood. The solutions, like the problem itself, are complex and difficult. They require skill, imagination, courage, and sound judgment.

Undoubtedly, this environmental design will mean that the scope of the high school will become more limited in the future. The National Commission on Youth does not believe that this is all bad. For too long the high school has carried the major burden for the transition of youth to adulthood. In today's complex society, no institution can be the measure of all things. No single institution can suffice as the exclusive environment for youth.

National Commitment to a New Environment

In an earlier period of national crisis, Thomas Paine observed that "danger and deliverance make their advances together; and it is only in the last push that one or the other takes the lead."

Presently, danger and deliverance lie not in the hands of youth but in the hands of those who control the socialization institutions in which youth operate – parents in the home environment, educators in the school environment, and employers in the community environment.

If new environments for the transition of youth to adulthood are to become a reality, new relationships that transcend traditional arrangements must be developed. The chasm between learning and earning in this country is wide, historic, and deep. Educators are frequently frightened by the means and motives of industry; employers are generally skeptical of the effectiveness of educational solutions to problems; and labor unions are traditionally suspicious of proposals by educators and employers alike.

Now, however, schools, labor, and industry must play an integral part in this effort to effect change. These old adversaries become new bedfellows. The National Commission on Youth is convinced that youth transitional planning councils (Chapter 4) can be the catalyst to forge the necessary linkages between the classroom and the workplace.

The problem is not one of means, but one of common ends. As a society, America has yet to follow the lead of other Western democracies in making a common national commitment to youth.

Until such time as a national commitment to youth is made in the form of a coherent policy, the negative trends that are documented in this report may be expected to continue.

Notes

1. Excerpted from a presentation by Willis W. Harman to the National Commission on Youth at Cornell University, Ithaca, N.Y., on May 11, 1977.
Also see Elise Boulding, "Learning to Make New Futures," Research for Better Schools, Inc., Philadelphia, Pa., February 1975, p. 4.
2. Boulding, "Learning," p. 6.
3. Remarks made by Urie Bronfenbrenner to the National Commission on Youth at Cornell University, Ithaca, N.Y., on May 11, 1977 (transcribed).
4. Bruno Bettelheim, "The Family Then and Now," *New York University Education Quarterly*, vol. 3, no. 3, spring 1977, p. 5.
5. Ralph W. Tyler, "Tomorrow's Education," *American Education*, August-September 1975, p. 17.
6. John R. Silber, "The Pollution of Time," commencement address, Boston University, Boston, Mass., May 23, 1971.
7. Edward Wynne, "Schools That Serve Families," *The National Elementary Principal*, vol. 55, no. 6, July-August 1976, p. 9.
8. The concept of the transition school was proposed by U.S. Commissioner of Education Ernest W. Boyer in a speech to the American Jewish Committee, April 17, 1978.
See also Ernest W. Boyer, "Commissioner's Model for the 1980's," *New York Times*, Sunday, January 7, 1979, sec. 13, p. 14.
9. James S. Coleman, *How Do the Young Become Adults?*, Center for Social Reorganization of Schools, Report no. 130, The Johns Hopkins University, Baltimore, Md., 1972, p. 12.
10. An excellent comprehensive analysis of the secularization of youth is contained in Willis W. Harman, *Citizenship Education and the Future*, U.S. Department of Health, Education and Welfare, Publication no. (OE)78-07006, 1978.
11. "Schools Get Half of YEDPA Funds," *Education U.S.A.*, December 11, 1978, p. 118.
12. The parameters of the current debate on vocational education can be seen in Everett Egginton, "Is Vocational Education Meeting Its Objectives?" *Phi Delta Kappan*, vol. 59, no. 8, April 1978, and Gordon I. Swenson, "Vocational Education: Fact and Fantasy," *Phi Delta Kappan*, vol. 60, no. 2, October 1978.
13. Coleman, *How Do the Young Become Adults?*, p. 15.
14. Stephen F. Hamilton, "Experiental Learning Programs for Youth," study prepared for the National Institute of Education, June 1978, Cornell University.
Also see Ellen Greenberger and Lawrence D. Steinberg, "Early Adolescents

at Work: Effects of Part-Time Employment on Literacy and Maturity," Program in Social Ecology, University of California, Irvine, 1978.

15. Richard H. Dollase, "Action Learning: Its Anticipated and Unanticipated Consequences," *The Clearing House*, vol. 52, no. 3, November 1978, p. 103.

12
TOWARD A NATIONAL POLICY
FOR YOUTH

Recommendation 26: A Presidential Commission to Study Youth Problems. *A presidential commission should be established to study the social, economic, and political conditions from which arise the problems of youth. Focusing on these larger issues, the recommendations of the commission would serve as a philosophical anchor point for Congress to legislate specific laws and mechanisms to facilitate the transition of youth to adulthood.*

Recommendation 27: A White House Youth Office to Coordinate Policies and Programs. *A White House youth office should be established to coordinate more effectively the present horizontal approach to policy-making and program implementation. Operating under presidential mandate, the youth office would be empowered to coordinate all youth-related policies, programs, and budgetary decisions. This vertical dimension should result in more effective decision-making procedures and give much-needed visibility to youth affairs on the national level.*

If one searched Washington, D.C., for *the* youth policy of the nation and *the* process by which it is made, one would search in vain. Instead, one would discover a plethora of youth policies and practices masquerading as a national youth policy. It is clearly evident to the National Commission on Youth that the bits and pieces of youth policy are, in John Gardner's phrase, "lying all around needing to be assembled."

At the present time, youth policy is concocted by at least eight cabinet departments—Health, Education and Welfare; Labor; Justice; Commerce; Interior; Housing and Urban Development; Agriculture; and Defense. Practically every federal agency provides some type of funding or service assistance for programs that have real or potential youth impact. Further, countless government policies and practices, ranging from personal and business taxation policies to executive management and budgetary decisions, have far-reaching indirect impact on youth.

In addition to the number of agencies involved in making youth policy, overlapping and, on occasion, conflicting jurisdictions exacerbate the problem. To cite one example, at the moment over twenty federal government and private agencies are focusing their efforts on improving the transition of youth from the school into jobs.[1] They include agencies that administer youth programs, agencies that confine their efforts to program and planning advice, agencies that conduct youth-related research, and agencies that function as advocates for youth. Countless other examples could be cited. The inescapable conclusion remains: the information on which policy is made is often limited, fragmentary, and even at odds. It is hardly surprising, therefore, that the Congress has not been able to formulate a national youth policy that is bold, imaginative, and comprehensive in scope.

Yet, in another sense, such facts serve to refute the observation that America does not have a national youth policy. It does. But it is a policy that is incoherent and inexplicit, a policy that is skewed by contradictions and inconsistencies, a policy that is more often than not evolved in response to crises, a policy that consists mainly of a collection of short-term palliatives, and a policy that has never been exposed to prolonged and intensive scrutiny by either the government or the public.

The lack of a coherent national youth policy, notes Stephen Bailey, "is killing the natural idealism of American youth, robbing them of any sense of usefulness and purpose, and depriving this country of a vigor and vision it desperately needs."[2]

Lack of Political Power

The reasons for the lack of a national policy for youth are easily discerned. Foremost of all, youth have no political clout. This stems from several factors. First is the political apathy of youth as contrasted, say, with the political activism of the elderly. Admittedly, a large segment of youth are not eligible for the franchise by virtue of age. But the dismal voting record of those who are eligible to vote is signal testimony that young people are not political advocates for themselves.

Coupled with this lack of political power is a thinly veiled antiyouth attitude that currently exists in this country. This atavistic product of the turbulent decade of the 1960s is best observed from historical perspective. When Franklin D. Roosevelt developed the National Youth Administration in the 1930s, its budget consumed 7 percent of the total federal budget; today, by comparison, youth-related expenditures represent less than 1 percent of the federal budget.[3] From a financial standpoint, the national government has moved steadily backward from the idealism and commitment that it had toward young people during the Depression era.

Contrast this with the situation that prevails in Europe. As pointed out in Chapter 10, many European industrial democracies have made high-level policy decisions that grant youth priority status in national planning schemes. Most of these nations recognize that the needs of young people must be taken seriously if the future of the country and the prevailing political ideology is to be preserved. In America, however, there is precious little debate on national youth policy: there is no attempt to assess what currently exists as youth "policy"; there is even less analysis of what youth policy should be for the future.

The present situation is not without a touch of irony. Titanic policy struggles are waged on the floor of Congress on the future course of our national energy policy. Debates occur in every session of the Congress over a future national health policy. But what can be more important to the future health and the continued vitality of the republic than the care and upbringing of the next generation of leaders?

One thing seems certain. The nation will pay a high price at some future point for its present intransigence on youth policy. If large numbers of young people remain apathetic, cynical, and alienated to a political system that treats them so shabbily, it is not likely that as adults they will be strong supporters of the system.

Robert Dahl, the noted political scientist, once suggested that government decisions do not stem from "a majestic march of great majorities" but from "the relentless appeasement of powerful groups." Appeals to altruism no longer work. Youth must compete with other groups in our pluralistic society for leverage on government policy decisions. Public debate must be joined, and joined at every level of decision making. Starting at the very highest levels of policymaking and extending down to towns and neighborhoods, the needs and interests of youth need advocacy and representation. Without such representation, young people cannot compete equitably with all other segments of the populace for a fair share of our national resources and opportunities.

Allies and advocates for youth must be recruited in all shapes and sizes—youth themselves, parents, teachers, social workers, government officials, and the voluntary sector, along with all others who share a common belief in young people. The realities are simple but formidable. Until such coalitions succeed in raising youth policy to a priority level, young people will continue to be consigned to the "cheap seats" in the rear of the political arena.

Policy Planning in a Pluralistic Society

Another explanation for the lack of a national youth policy is more philosophical in nature. It rests on the tendency in democratic societies to place individual interests over those of the mass. In Soviet-style coercive planning, national goals are simply imposed from above. Free from the forces that operate in a market economy, the preferences of the planners are substituted for those of the public. As a result, a whole variety of costs can be built into the budget at the administrative level for such things as training young people for jobs.

In sharp contrast to this approach, in the United States, policy-making is a much more unwieldly process. Attempts are usually made to elicit public preferences on issues through the usual channels of public discussion and consultation with assorted interest groups. Policy is then thrashed out through legislative action.

When one adds to this the administrative burdens of implementing and supervising public policies on a national scale, it is understandable that there are not easy solutions.[4] Program costs and unacceptable economic trade-offs such as inflation and adult unemployment tend to blunt efforts to develop successful youth policies. Adding to these difficulties is the presence of numerous parties involved in the decision-making process: federal, state, and local governments; educators; employers; and parents. And youth themselves must necessarily play a role in policy and program decisions.

The multiple difficulties, however, do not negate the case for consideration of a national youth policy. They only make it harder. The fragmentation that follows as a by-product of making policy from "below rather than from above" is not only inevitable but even to some extent desirable.[5] It is, in short, the price a democratic society pays for its liberty and individualism.

A Call for a Comprehensive Youth Policy

Considering the depth and the breadth of the problems confronting young people in America today, the National Commission on Youth is convinced that a national youth policy is necessary, advisable, and long overdue. The practice of making youth policy only in response to crisis must end. The net result of this approach has been a fragmented collection of short-term palliatives, when what is sorely needed is a national ongoing policy directed at the problems of youth.

The quest must begin on the following assumption: many youth problems stem not from factors that are specific to youth but from broader problems endemic to society as a whole.[6] Youth problems in America are mostly symptoms of problems embedded deeply in the political, social, and economic fabric of the nation. As such, the symptoms will disappear only through fundamental systematic change.

If this is a valid view, the policy that is proposed cannot be yet another collection of fragmented partial solutions. What is needed instead is a broadly based approach that confronts issues of fundamental consequence.[7] For example, if a National Youth Service is a good concept, what threat, real or perceived, does this pose to the employment of aged and unskilled workers? If educational reform seems needed, why is there less willingness in society to pay for public education? If serious private-sector involvement is in line with long-term resolutions to the problems of youth, what steps must be taken to reduce negative incentives and improve positive incentives such as wage subsidies, training-program grants, and postponement of wage taxes? If the voluntary sector is to play a crucial role in this process, what laws regulating philanthropic foundations must be changed in order to encourage their assistance? These, along with a host of similar questions, must be raised and resolved on a continuing basis if any proposed national youth policy is to be more than marginally effective.

Putting the Pieces Together

The call for action comes easily. Analysis, development, and implementation of policy do not.

Any call for a national youth policy raises a number of questions: What is the most fruitful manner in which to raise and to analyze the fundamental issues associated with a national youth policy? How does one begin to put together the various bits and pieces that masquerade at the present time as youth policy? How can the needs of youth be raised to priority status? What are the ways to give greater coherence and articulation to youth policy?

Government has never been very articulate and straightforward in response to these questions. What can be done? The National Commission on Youth believes that there are some obvious steps that the federal government must take. They are not difficult or expensive. They are measures that should have been taken long ago.

Presidential Commission on Youth

The National Commission on Youth recommends the creation of a presidential commission to study the problems of youth. However, the members of the National Commission on Youth harbor no illusions about the future of yet another presidential commission. The Commissioners are well aware that monuments are erected to the deeds of individuals, not to commissions.

All too often in the past presidential commissions have been utilized to create the illusion of change, to sidestep critical issues, or simply to postpone difficult decisions. In far too many instances, short-term simplistic "solutions" have been recommended out of political timidity, only to gather dust on library shelves.

Prevailing political wisdom maintains that the only way to stave off crisis is through compromise and concession to interest groups and acceptance of whatever is politically feasible. Admittedly, this is good rhetoric and has a pragmatic ring to it. But the result is the passage of an assorted witches' brew of piecemeal programs to mollify the various interest groups. Ultimately, such temporizing only brings the nation a step closer to the flash point of crisis.

It must be recognized that youth problems are primarily symptoms of larger problems that exist in the social, economic, and political environment. Thus, solutions to the problems of youth can only be found by attacks on the larger problems of which they are a part.

A presidential commission that is willing to assume this task will have considerable merit. It will not be easy. Considerable courage is required to bring about long-term and basic changes in the social, economic, and political environment. The commission's recommendations could serve as a philosophic base from which the Congress could legislate specific laws and mechanisms to attack the problems of youth. Finally, the commission's work, through the Office of the President, would elevate the visibility of youth issues to a status they presently do not have.

One point needs to be emphasized. Until there is a willingness to confront the more basic problems behind the symptoms, there will be no national youth policy. The nation will continue to be plagued with the unnecessary task of debating burning questions that have been debated endlessly in the past with few, if any, discernible results. When rhetoric at long last ebbs, present realities remain. To these realities the National Commission on Youth now turns its attention.

White House Youth Office

Presently, most government youth policies and services are based on a symptom-specific approach. Typically, this approach operates according to the following scenario: Departmental jurisdiction is established according to the observed symptoms – crime and delinquency are funneled into the Justice Department, unemployment into Labor, environmental work projects into Interior, and so on. Then various offices and agencies within departments are charged with formulating policies and prescribing "treatments" for the problem or symptom. While preserving institutional autonomy, such vertical arrangements invariably produce more heat than light in the policymaking process.

Collaboration among youth-serving agencies is further impeded by the tendency to shape policy that deals with only parts of the transitional process: the transition to jobs, the educational system, juvenile crime, the health needs of young people, and so on. The fragmentation is exacerbated further as youth policy is implemented through carefully guarded jurisdictional boundaries. The conventional view from Washington is that the federal government should provide funding, overview, and oversight, but that implementation and experimentation are best left to states and local communities. The result is that policy is usually made after the fact, based on the evaluation of local initiatives. Herein lies the major difference between European and American approaches to youth policy: Europeans, while encouraging local flexibility, deal at the national level with policymaking and implementation.[8]

The Commission views the present piecemeal approach to policymaking as self-defeating. It is unrealistic to expect that the literally hundreds of policies and programs that have been concocted over the years can be effectively coordinated. The present forces of institutional separation are so powerful that youth policy is usually made in splendid isolation. The Office of Youth Development within the Department of Health, Education and Welfare has failed as a coordinating mechanism. Lacking both visibility and sufficient mandate, the youth development office is unable to coordinate youth affairs even within its own department.

While the National Commission on Youth questions the effectiveness of many existing policies and programs, nonetheless their reality cannot be escaped. If youth problems cannot be solved through such a mixture of uncoordinated programs directed at the symptom-problems of youth, what kinds of action are needed?

The inclination to recommend a department of youth affairs is strong, but it is neither timely nor possible. Unless all youth-related programs were removed from their present departmental jurisdictions, which hardly seems likely, a new youth department would provide merely a costly illusion of reform.

Then there are the political realities of such a proposal. Any call for a separate youth department would immediately spark similar demands from a host of special-interest groups including women, children, and the aged.

There are some steps that government can take that do not require an extensive new bureaucracy. Specifically, the National Commission on Youth recommends the creation of an office of youth affairs within the White House. Operating along the lines of the present Office of Management and Budget, it would transcend departmental fiefdoms and serve as the coordinating mechanism for now disparate programs and policies. Youth-related issues would immediately receive new status and visibility. Operating under presidential mandate, an office of youth affairs would be given oversight status and be empowered to call together government departments for purposes of coordinating youth-related budgets and policies. Most important of all, by operating out of the executive branch instead of one or more of the various departments, youth policies could be coordinated more effectively than the present setup. The needs of youth would be afforded direct, immediate, and continuous access to the president.

It must be emphasized that the creation of an office of youth affairs would not, by itself, solve all of the problems of formulating a coherent youth policy. But a new horizontal approach to policy-making is infinitely preferable to the present unwieldly vertical structure.

Youth Policy in the Balance

The Youth Employment and Demonstration Projects Act (YEDPA), signed into law by President Carter on August 5, 1977, represents movement on the part of the administration to create new environments for youth. Designed to serve a broad spectrum of the youth population, the measure provides opportunities to acquire job skills, gives youth a chance to perform socially useful work in communities, and assists poorly prepared youth to increase their education while being productively employed. If fully funded and implemented, YEDPA can be a significant first step toward a coherent national youth policy.

But the process must not stop here. Something more fundamental is necessary. Unless a way is found to bring about change in some of the more basic problems affecting the relationship between the public and private sectors, tinkering with bits and pieces of youth policies and programs will be of little avail. A long and hard look must be taken at those laws, policies, programs, and institutional arrangements that show little or no evidence of improving the reward and penalty systems with which youth must grow up.

All this represents a radical departure from the past in which policies were developed in reaction to crisis. The need is not to establish more special or emergency programs; rather, the need is to create a comprehensive and continuous national policy for youth.

Much, of course, will depend on presidential initiative. The basic commitment must be made in the public realm. But presidents are not the only movers and shakers. The Congress, with its vast prescriptive capacities; the courts, from which important policy directives on youth have emerged in the past decade; the high schools, which must teach youth intellectual skills; the corporate sector, which must provide most of the jobs for youth; voluntary associations, with their special kinds of expertise on the problems of youth; and state and local governments, which confront the problems of youth on a daily basis must all play key roles in the policymaking process.

The degree of interdependence among government, the courts, the schools, and the private sector has increased tremendously in recent times. Without question, this interdependence greatly determines the climate of the environment in which youth grow to adulthood.

It is one thing to say that such interdependence exists, but the full implications are far from understood, even by those making youth policy. The National Commission on Youth believes that there is an urgent need to probe these relationships. Studies need to be made of the institutional interdependence among such entities as the courts, the legislature, the schools, and private business and industry. The assumption underlying this recommendation is that policy studies of this nature will ultimately strengthen the insight of all of these institutions that exercise such powerful leverage on the environments in which youth mature.

A Turning Point?

Each day it becomes clearer that the nation stands poised at a turning point of decision where the fate of youth policy hangs in the balance. What is done or is not done in the next few years will determine whether this was the beginning of a significant new era for youth or just another turning point in history when history failed to turn.

Until there is a willingness to tackle the basic issues that have been presented in this report, there will be no redirection in the present trend. The longer the vacillation on these issues and the greater the procrastination on policy directives, the more the nation is confronted by the tyranny of time and decision.

Undeniably, this is a time of crisis for youth in America. It is also a time of unparalleled opportunity to deal with the issues that make for crisis. This report has documented the former; its recommendations are offered in the spirit of the latter.

Notes

1. Marcia Freedman, "Youth Employment in the United States: An Outline of the Issues," September 24, 1976 (mimeographed), p. 13.

2. Stephen K. Bailey, *Service Learning for the Future: Domestic and International Programs*, Policy Analysis Service, American Council on Education, Washington, D.C., January 1978, p. V.

3. Bernard E. Anderson, *Youth Unemployment*, Hearing before the Joint Economic Committee, Congress of the United States, Ninety-fourth Cong., September 9, 1976 (U.S. Government Printing Office, Washington, D.C.), p. 96.

4. Paul E. Barton, "Youth Transition to Work: The Problem and Federal Policy Setting," *From School to Work: Improving the Transition*, a collection of policy papers prepared for the National Commission for Manpower Policy (U.S. Government Printing Office, Washington, D.C., 1975), p. 5.

Also see Stephen K. Bailey, "Education, Jobs, and Community Services: What Directions for National Policies?" in Ralph W. Tyler, ed., *From Youth to Constructive Adult Life: The Role of the Public School* (McCutchan Publishing Corporation, Berkeley, Calif., 1978), pp. 93-94.

5. A.G. Watts, "A Policy For Youth?" *The Ditchley Journal*, spring 1977, p. 35.

6. Ibid., p. 36.

7. Excerpted from a presentation by Willis W. Harman to the National Commission on Youth at Cornell University, Ithaca, N.Y., on May 11, 1977.

8. Freedman, "Youth Employment," p. 13.

APPENDIX A

SCHEDULE OF TESTIMONY

SCHEDULE OF TESTIMONY
NATIONAL COMMISSION ON YOUTH

O'Hare Hilton, Chicago, Illinois, December 10, 1976

NAME	TOPIC	REPRESENTING
Ms. Kathy Garmezy	Developments in Municipal Youth Policy	National League of Cities/U.S. Conference of Mayors
Dr. Edward Wynne	Socialization to Adulthood	Department of Policy Studies, University of Illinois at Chicago Circle

Miami Marriott, Miami, Florida, February 8, 1977

NAME	TOPIC	REPRESENTING
Mr. Donald J. Eberly	National Service for Youth: Pros and Cons of Compulsory Versus Volunteer Service	National Service Secretariat
The Hon. Peter B. Edelman	State Policy on Youth: What It Is at Present and What It Should Be	New York State Division for Youth
Dr. Sar A. Levitan	The Extent of Youth Unemployment and Some Possible Solutions	Center for Social Policy Studies, The George Washington University
Dr. Beatrice G. Reubens	A National Policy on Youth From an Economist's Viewpoint	Conservation of Human Resources, Columbia University
Mr. Levi Wilson, Jr.	Problems of Youth in Dade County, Florida	Department of Human Resources, Manpower Administration Division

Statler Inn, Cornell University, Ithaca, New York, May 11, 1977

NAME	TOPIC	REPRESENTING
Dr. William R. Buechner	The Implications for Youth in Pending Legislation	Joint Economic Committee, United States Congress
Dr. Robert M. Hunter	A Youth Services System and National Strategy for Youth Development	Center for Action Research, Inc.

Sheraton Carlton, Washington, D.C., September 15-16, 1977

NAME	TOPIC	REPRESENTING
Dr. Roy H. Forbes	Gaps in the Knowledge of Youth	National Assessment of Educational Progress
Mr. John M. Greacen	Youth and Crime	Police Foundation
Ms. Emily Martin	Youth and Crime	Office of Juvenile Justice and Delinquency Prevention
Dr. Jacob Mincer	The Negative Effects of the Minimum Wage on Youth	Department of Economics, Columbia University
The Hon. Albert H. Quie	A Minimum Wage Concept for Youth	Education and Labor Committee, United States House of Representatives
Dr. James F. Ragan, Jr.	The Impact of the Minimum Wage on Youth Employment	Business Conditions Division, Federal Reserve Bank of New York
Dr. Gilbert Schiffman	Gaps in the Knowledge of Youth	Right to Read Program

O'Hare Hilton, Chicago, Illinois, December 16, 1977

NAME	TOPIC	REPRESENTING
Dr. James Coleman	What Are Appropriate Environments in Which Youth Can Best Grow Into Adults?	Department of Sociology, University of Chicago
Mr. Walter Davis	Labor's View of Programs for Youth	AFL-CIO
Mr. Dennis Gallagher	New Prospects for Youth: Worlds of Education, Work, and Service	National Manpower Institute
Dr. George Gallup	What the New Gallup Youth Polls Have Learned About Youth	American Institute of Public Opinion
Dr. Robert T. McGee	What the Schools Can Do	Denton (Texas) Independent School District
Mrs. Mildred K. Wurf	Direct Service and Advocacy by National Voluntary Youth-Serving Organizations	National Collaboration for Youth

The Mayflower, Washington, D.C., March 2, 1978

NAME	TOPIC	REPRESENTING
Mr. Larry Dye	HEW Plans for Youth Programs and Activities	Youth Development Program, Department of Health, Education, and Welfare
Dr. Richard L. Ferguson	What American College Testing Has Learned About Youth	Research and Development Division, The American College Testing Program
Mr. Sidney L. Johnson	Syracuse National Youth Demonstration Project	Syracuse (New York) City School District
Mr. David M. Muchnick	ACTION's Programs for Youth	ACTION National Youth Service
Mr. Robert Taggart III	U.S. Department of Labor Youth Programs	Office of Youth Programs, Employment and Training Administration, United States Department of Labor

The Mayflower, Washington, D.C., April 27-28, 1978

NAME	TOPIC	REPRESENTING
Mr. Governor Aker	The Youth Conservation Corps	Youth Programs, United States Department of the Interior
Mrs. Grace Baisinger	Impact of Television on Youth As Viewed by the PTA	National PTA
Mr. William Hewitt	Report on Organization for Economic Cooperation and Development (OECD) Conference on Youth Unemployment, Paris	Office of Policy, Evaluation, and Research, Employment and Training Administration, United States Department of Labor
Mr. A. Sidney Johnson III Ms. Theodora Ooms	Family Impact on Youth	Family Impact Seminar, Institute for Educational Leadership, The George Washington University
Mr. Frank Jones	Model Health Programs for Youth	Robert Wood Johnson Foundation
Dr. Charles U. Lowe	Health Problems of Youth	Office of Child Health Affairs, Department of Health, Education, and Welfare

APPENDIX B

SURVEY OF YOUTH POLICY IN THE STATES AND TERRITORIES

NATIONAL COMMISSION ON YOUTH
SURVEY OF YOUTH POLICY
IN THE STATES AND TERRITORIES

Policy Classifications

State or Territory	Delinquency Related Programs	Education Centered Programs	Youth Advocacy Programs	Miscellaneous Programs	Comprehensive Programs
Alabama					
Alaska	●				
Arizona					
Arkansas	●				
California	●		●		
Colorado				●	
Connecticut	●				
Delaware					
Florida	●	●			
Georgia	●				
Hawaii			●		
Idaho					
Illinois			●		
Indiana			●		
Iowa			●		
Kansas			●		
Kentucky					

Policy Classifications

State or Territory	Delinquency Related Programs	Education Centered Programs	Youth Advocacy Programs	Miscellaneous Programs	Comprehensive Programs
Louisiana	●		●		
Maine			●		
Maryland					
Massachusetts		●	●		
Michigan	●				
Minnesota					
Mississippi	●				
Missouri			●		
Montana					●
Nebraska					
Nevada			●		
New Hampshire			●		
New Jersey		●		●	
New Mexico			●		
New York	●				
North Carolina			●		
North Dakota	●				

Policy Classifications

State or Territory	Delinquency Related Programs	Education Centered Programs	Youth Advocacy Programs	Miscellaneous Programs	Comprehensive Programs
Ohio	●				
Oklahoma					
Oregon			●		
Pennsylvania					●
Rhode Island			●		
South Carolina			●		
South Dakota					
Tennessee			●		
Texas			●		
Utah				●	
Vermont			●		
Virginia			●		
Washington	●				
West Virginia	●				
Wisconsin	●				
Wyoming			●		
American Samoa			●		
Guam					
Puerto Rico		●			
Virgin Islands			●		

INDEX

World Health Organization, 121, 124

Wyoming, 156

YAC. *See* Youth Activities Commission

YACC. *See* Young Adult Conservation Corps

YCC. *See* Youth Conservation Corps

YCSP. *See* Youth Community Service project

YEDPA. *See* Youth Employment and Demonstration Projects Act

YES. *See* Youth Employment Subsidy

YMCA. *See* Young Men's Christian Association

Young Adult Conservation Corps (YACC), 44

Young Men's Christian Association (YMCA), 28

Young Women's Christian Association (YWCA), 28

Youth, 9, 14. *See also* Age grading

Youth Activities Commission (YAC), 135–137

Youth advocacy programs, 153–156

Youth Camps (New York state), 152

Youth Community Conservation and Improvement Project, 44

Youth Community Service project (YCSP), 44, 58

Youth Conservation Corps (YCC), 42

Youth Development Centers (New York state), 152

Youth Employment and Demonstration Projects Act (YEDPA) of 1977, 43–44, 93, 193, 206

Youth Employment Subsidy (YES), 167

Youth Employment Training Program, 44

Youth Incentive Entitlement Projects, 44

Youth Motivation Task Force, 26

Youth Services Division (Portland, Oregon), 140–142

Youth transitional planning councils, 3, 5, 6, 63, 64–73, 188, 196

Youth: Transition to Adulthood, 12

Youth-tutoring-youth program, 27

YWCA. *See* Young Women's Christian Association